THE ENCYCLOPEDIA OF PSYCHOACTIVE DRUGS

IN 25 VOLUMES
Each title on a specific drug or drug-related problem

QUAALUDES

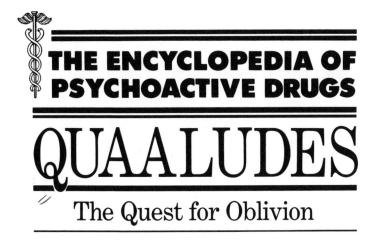

THE ENCYCLOPEDIA OF PSYCHOACTIVE DRUGS

QUAALUDES

The Quest for Oblivion

MARILYN CARROLL, Ph.D.

University of Minnesota Medical School

GARY GALLO

University of Minnesota Medical School

1985
CHELSEA HOUSE PUBLISHERS
NEW YORK

SENIOR EDITOR: William P. Hansen
ASSOCIATE EDITORS: John Haney, Richard Mandell
CAPTIONS EDITOR: Marian W. Taylor
EDITORIAL COORDINATOR: Karyn Gullen Browne
ART DIRECTOR: Susan Lusk
LAYOUT: Carol McDougall
ART ASSISTANTS: Ghila Krajzman, Tenaz Mehta
PICTURE RESEARCH: Susan Quist
COVER: "The Sleepers III," George Tooker, 1976

First Printing

Library of Congress Cataloging in Publication Data
Carroll, Marilyn.
    Quaaludes: the quest for oblivion.
    (The Encyclopedia of psychoactive drugs)
    Bibliography: p.
    Includes index.
    Summary: Examines the nature, effects, and medical
and legal aspects of methaqualone use and abuse.
    1.   Methaqualone abuse—Juvenile literature.
2. Methaqualone—Juvenile literature.   [1. Methaqualone.
2. Drugs.   3. Drug abuse]   I. Gallo, Gary.   II. Title.
III. Series.
RC568.M45C37   1985   616.86'3   85–11043

ISBN 0-87754-766-1

Chelsea House Publishers
Harold Steinberg, Chairman & Publisher
Susan Lusk, Vice President
A Division of Chelsea House Educational Communications, Inc.

Chelsea House Publishers
133 Christopher Street
New York, NY 10014

Photos courtesy of AP/Wide World Photos, *High Times,* Holt, Rinehart &
Winston, *Library Journal, Miami Herald*/Joe Rimkus, Jr., National Archives,
Phoenix House, UPI/Bettmann Newsphotos, and U.S. Drug Enforcement Agency.

CONTENTS

A suspected drug dealer stands handcuffed as members of federal and state narcotics task forces search his trailer home for methaqualone and other illegal drugs. To prevent other dealers from recognizing the suspect, his appearance in the photograph has been altered.

FOREWORD

In the Mainstream of American Life

The rapid growth of drug use and abuse is one of the most dramatic changes in the fabric of American society in the last 20 years. The United States has the highest level of psychoactive drug use of any industrialized society. It is 10 to 30 times greater than it was 20 years ago.

According to a recent Gallup poll, young people consider drugs the leading problem that they face. One of the legacies of the social upheaval of the 1960s is that psychoactive drugs have become part of the mainstream of American life. Schools, homes, and communities cannot be "drug proofed." There is a demand for drugs—and the supply is plentiful. Social norms have changed and drugs are not only available—they are everywhere.

Almost all drug use begins in the preteen and teenage years. These years are few in the total life cycle, but critical in the maturation process. During these years adolescents face the difficult tasks of discovering their identity, clarifying their sexual roles, asserting their independence, learning to cope with authority, and searching for goals that will give their lives meaning. During this intense period of growth, conflict is inevitable and the temptation to use drugs is great. Drugs are readily available, adolescents are curious and vulnerable, there is peer pressure to experiment, and there is the temptation to escape from conflicts.

No matter what their age or socioeconomic status, no group is immune to the allure and effects of psychoactive drugs. The U.S. Surgeon General's report, "Healthy People," indicates that 30% of all deaths in the United States

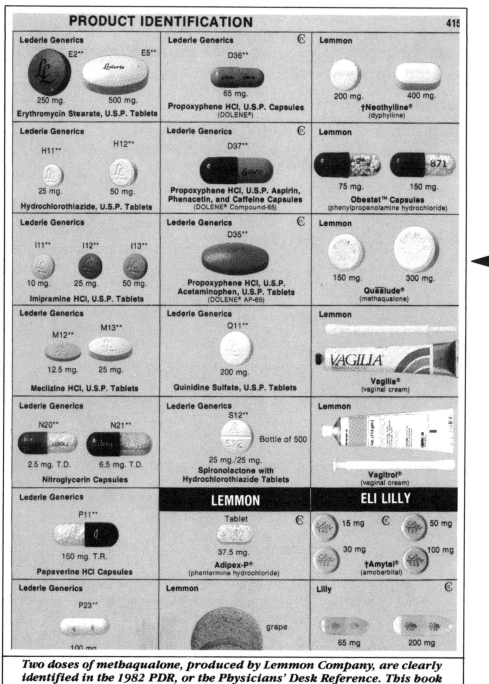

PRODUCT IDENTIFICATION 415

Lederle Generics
E2** | E5**
250 mg. | 500 mg.
Erythromycin Stearate, U.S.P. Tablets

Lederle Generics ℞
D36**
65 mg.
Propoxyphene HCl, U.S.P. Capsules
(DOLENE®)

Lemmon
200 mg. | 400 mg.
†Neothylline®
(dyphylline)

Lederle Generics
H11** | H12**
25 mg. | 50 mg.
Hydrochlorothiazide, U.S.P. Tablets

Lederle Generics ℞
D37**
Propoxyphene HCl, U.S.P. Aspirin,
Phenacetin, and Caffeine Capsules
(DOLENE® Compound-65)

Lemmon
871
75 mg. | 150 mg.
Obestat™ Capsules
(phenylpropanolamine hydrochloride)

Lederle Generics
I11** | I12** | I13**
10 mg. | 25 mg. | 50 mg.
Imipramine HCl, U.S.P. Tablets

Lederle Generics ℞
D35**
Propoxyphene HCl, U.S.P.
Acetaminophen, U.S.P. Tablets
(DOLENE® AP-65)

Lemmon
150 mg. | 300 mg.
Quāālude®
(methaqualone)

Lederle Generics
M12** | M13**
12.5 mg. | 25 mg.
Meclizine HCl, U.S.P. Tablets

Lederle Generics
Q11**
200 mg.
Quinidine Sulfate, U.S.P. Tablets

Lemmon
VAGILIA
Vagilia®
(vaginal cream)

Lederle Generics
N20** | N21**
2.5 mg. T.D. | 6.5 mg. T.D.
Nitroglycerin Capsules

Lederle Generics
S12**
Bottle of 500
25 mg./25 mg.
Spironolactone with
Hydrochlorothiazide Tablets

Lemmon
Vagitrol®
(vaginal cream)

Lederle Generics
P11**
150 mg. T.R.
Papaverine HCl Capsules

LEMMON
Tablet ℞
37.5 mg.
Adipex-P®
(phentermine hydrochloride)

ELI LILLY
15 mg ℞ | 50 mg
30 mg | 100 mg
†Amytal®
(amobarbital)

Lederle Generics
P23**
100 mg

Lemmon
grape

Lilly ℞
65 mg | 200 mg

Two doses of methaqualone, produced by Lemmon Company, are clearly identified in the 1982 PDR, or the Physicians' Desk Reference. This book is an important source of information about all available drugs.

are premature because of alcohol and tobacco use. However, the most shocking development in this report is that mortality in the age group between 15 and 24 has increased since 1960 despite the fact that death rates for all other age groups have declined in the 20th century. Accidents, suicides, and homicides are the leading cause of death in young people 15 to 24 years of age. In many cases the deaths are directly related to drug use.

THE ENCYCLOPEDIA OF PSYCHOACTIVE DRUGS answers the questions that young people are likely to ask about drugs, as well as those they might not think to ask, but should. Topics include: what it means to be intoxicated; how drugs affect mood; why people take drugs; who takes them; when they take them; and how much they take. They will learn what happens to a drug when it enters the body. They will learn what it means to get "hooked" and how it happens. They will learn how drugs affect their driving, their school work, and those around them—their peers, their family, their friends, and their employers. They will learn what the signs are that indicate that a friend or a family member may have a drug problem and to identify four stages leading from drug use to drug abuse. Myths about drugs are dispelled.

National surveys indicate that students are eager for information about drugs and that they respond to it. Students not only need information about drugs—they want information. How they get it often proves crucial. Providing young people with accurate knowledge about drugs is one of the most critical aspects.

THE ENCYCLOPEDIA OF PSYCHOACTIVE DRUGS synthesizes the wealth of new information in this field and demystifies this complex and important subject. Each volume in the series is written by an expert in the field. Handsomely illustrated, this multi-volume series is geared for teenage readers. Young people will read these books, share them, talk about them, and make more informed decisions because of them.

Miriam Cohen, Ph.D.
Contributing Editor

A Drug Enforcement Agency technician demonstrates the operation of a tableting press. The lightweight, portable machine, which operates on house current or by hand, could produce up to 250 counterfeit Quaalude tablets a minute. Officials report that most of the methaqualone sold on the U.S. black market is processed in illegal Colombian labs.

INTRODUCTION

The Gift of Wizardry
Use and Abuse

JACK H. MENDELSON, M.D.
NANCY K. MELLO, PH.D.
Alcohol and Drug Abuse Research Center
Harvard Medical School—McLean Hospital

Dorothy to the Wizard:

"I think you are a very bad man," said Dorothy.
"Oh, no, my dear; I'm really a very good man; but I'm a very bad Wizard."
—from THE WIZARD OF OZ

Man is endowed with the gift of wizardry, a talent for discovery and invention. The discovery and invention of substances that change the way we feel and behave are among man's special accomplishments, and like so many other products of our wizardry, these substances have the capacity to harm as well as to help. The substance itself is neutral, an intricate molecular structure. Yet, "too much" can be sickening, even deadly. It is man who decides how each substance is used, and it is man's beliefs and perceptions that give this neutral substance the attributes to heal or destroy.

Consider alcohol—available to all and yet regarded with intense ambivalence from biblical times to the present day. The use of alcoholic beverages dates back to our earliest ancestors. Alcohol use and misuse became associated with the worship of gods and demons. One of the most powerful Greek gods was Dionysus, lord of the Underworld and god of wine. The Romans adopted Dionysus but changed his name to Bacchus. Festivals and holidays associated with Bacchus celebrated the harvest and the origins of life. Time has blurred the images of the Bacchanalian festival, but the theme of drunkenness as a major part of celebration has survived the pagan gods and remains a familiar part of modern society. The term "Bacchanalian festival" conveys a more appealing image than "drunken orgy" or "pot

13

party," but whatever the label, some of the celebrants will inevitably start up the "high" escalator to the next plateau. Once there, the de-escalation is difficult for many.

According to reliable estimates, one out of every ten Americans develops a serious alcohol-related problem sometime in his or her lifetime. In addition, automobile accidents caused by drunken drivers claim the lives of tens of thousands every year. Many of the victims are gifted young people, just starting out in adult life. Hospital emergency rooms abound with patients seeking help for alcohol-related injuries.

Who is to blame? Can we blame the many manufacturers who produce such an amazing variety of alcoholic beverages? Should we blame the educators who fail to explain the perils of intoxication, or so exaggerate the dangers of drinking that no one could possibly believe them? Are friends to blame—those peers who urge others to "drink more and faster," or the macho types who stress the importance of being able to "hold your liquor"? Casting blame, however, is hardly constructive, and pointing the finger is a fruitless way to deal with problems. Alcoholism and drug abuse have few culprits but many victims. Accountability begins with each of us, every time we choose to use or to misuse an intoxicating substance.

It is ironic that some of man's earliest medicines, derived from natural plant products, are used today to poison and to intoxicate. Relief from pain and suffering is one of society's many continuing goals. Over 3,000 years ago, the Therapeutic Papyrus of Thebes, one of our earliest written records, gave instructions for the use of opium in the treatment of pain. Opium, in the form of its major derivative, morphine, remains one of the most powerful drugs we have for pain relief. But opium, morphine, and similar compounds, such as heroin, have also been used by many to induce changes in mood and feeling. Another example of man's misuse of a natural substance is the coca leaf, which for centuries was used by the Indians of Peru to reduce fatigue and hunger. Its modern derivative, cocaine, has important medical use as a local anesthetic. Unfortunately, its increasing abuse in the 1980s has reached epidemic proportions.

The purpose of this series is to provide information about the nature and behavioral effects of alcohol and drugs, and the probable consequences of both their moderate use and abuse. The authors believe that up-to-date, objective information about alcohol and drugs will help readers make better decisions as to whether to use them or not. The information presented here (and in other books in this series) is based on many clinical and laboratory studies and observations by people from diverse walks of life.

Over the centuries, novelists, poets, and dramatists have provided us with many insights into the beneficial and problematic aspects of alcohol and drug use. Physicians, lawyers, biologists, psychologists, and social scientists have contributed to a better understanding of the causes and consequences of using these substances. The authors in this series have attempted to gather and condense all the latest information about drug use and abuse. They have also described the sometimes wide gaps in our knowledge and have suggested some new ways to answer many difficult questions.

One such question, for example, is how do alcohol and drug problems get started? And what is the best way to treat them when they do? Not too many years ago, alcoholics and drug abusers were regarded as evil, immoral, or both. It is now recognized that these persons suffer from very complicated diseases involving deep psychological and social problems. To understand how the disease begins and progresses, it is necessary to understand the nature of the substance, the behavior of the afflicted person, and the characteristics of the society or culture in which he lives.

The diagram below shows the interaction of these three factors. The arrows indicate that the substance not only affects the user personally, but the society as well. Society influences attitudes towards the substance, which in turn affect its availability. The substance's impact upon the society may support or discourage the use and abuse of that substance.

SUBSTANCE
(ALCOHOL OR DRUG)

PERSON — SOCIETY

Although many of the social environments we live in are very similar, some of the most subtle differences can strongly influence our thinking and behavior. Where we live, go to school and work, whom we discuss things with—all influence our opinions about drug use and misuse. Yet we also share certain commonly accepted beliefs that outweigh any differences in our attitudes. The authors in this series have tried to identify and discuss the central, most crucial issues concerning drug use and misuse.

Regrettably, man's wizardry in developing new substances in medical therapeutics has not always been paralleled by intelligent usage. Although we do know a great deal about the effects of alcohol and drugs, we have yet to learn how to impart that knowledge, especially to young adults.

Does it matter? What harm does it do to smoke a little pot or have a few beers? What is it like to be intoxicated? How long does it last? Will it make me feel really fine? Will it make me sick? What are the risks? These are but a few of the questions answered in this series, which, hopefully, will enable the reader to make wise decisions concerning the crucial issue of drugs.

Information sensibly acted upon can go a long way towards helping everyone develop his or her best self. As one keen and sensitive observer, Dr. Lewis Thomas, has said,

> *"There is nothing at all absurd about the human condition. We matter. It seems to me a good guess, hazarded by a good many people who have thought about it, that we may be engaged in the formation of something like a mind for the life of this planet. If this is so, we are still at the most primitive stage, still fumbling with language and thinking, but infinitely capacitated for the future. Looked at this way, it is remarkable that we've come as far as we have in so short a period, really no time at all as geologists measure time. We are the newest, the youngest, and the brightest thing around."*

After making the arrest, a Miami, Florida, narcotics team inspects the well-hidden and deserted building where a college professor had operated a flourishing illegal methaqualone laboratory.

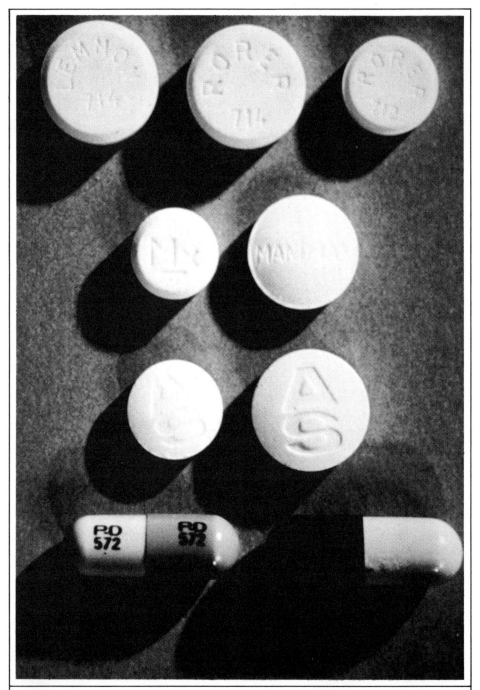

Methaqualone, marketed by several American and British drug companies, appeared in various forms and strengths. The Rorer company's Quaalude brand was the best known and the most often counterfeited.

CHAPTER 1

WHAT IS METHAQUALONE?

Methaqualone was first synthesized in India in 1955 by M.L. Gujral. Soon after, it was introduced and widely used in Europe and Japan as a "nonaddicting" hypnotic (sleeping pill). In the United States it was first manufactured in 1965 by the William H. Rorer pharmaceutical company under the trade name Quaalude (which soon became the common name for this whole category of drugs), and by 1972 it had become the nation's sixth-best-selling sedative/hypnotic. Many other pharmaceutical companies soon entered the methaqualone market when they saw how popular the drug was. The companies and the trade names they gave to methaqualone are Arnar-Stone (Sopor), Wallace (Optimil), Parke-Davis (Parest), and Smith, Miller, and Patch (Somnofac). In England methaqualone was marketed under the trade names Melsedrin, Tuazolone, and Mandrax (a combination of methaqualone and diphenhydramine, an antihistamine).

When methaqualone was introduced in the United States as a prescription drug for patients with sleep difficulties, it was not subject to controls of the Bureau of Narcotics and Dangerous Drugs (BNDD) as were other similar sedative/hypnotics, such as the barbiturates. Methaqualone was initially thought to be much safer than these drugs and to provide all of their advantages without their disadvantages or side effects. However, as methaqualone use increased, the risks associated with it became apparent.

In 1966 there were reports of methaqualone dependence characterized by a severe withdrawal. By 1968 there were reports of toxicity, overdose, and death resulting from misuse of methaqualone. The medical community began to question whether or not methaqualone provided any advantage over the drugs that preceded it. As early as April 22, 1966, the *Medical Letter* suggested that the claims for methaqualone (i.e., minimal side effects, rapid sleep induction, no hangover, and no addicting properties) were not supported by medical evidence.

Before the 1960s barbiturates were considered to be the most effective drugs for use as surgical anesthetics, and to treat tetanus, to reduce muscle contractions during electroconvulsive shock therapy, to immobilize the patient, and to reduce discomfort during certain x-ray procedures and during cataract surgery. However, barbiturates are dangerous because they suppress *all* bodily functions, even the ability of the patient to breathe.

When used repeatedly barbiturates can produce tolerance (which means greater amounts of a drug are needed to produce the desired effect) and physical dependence (characterized by illness or withdrawal symptoms when drug-taking is terminated). Even under the best surgical

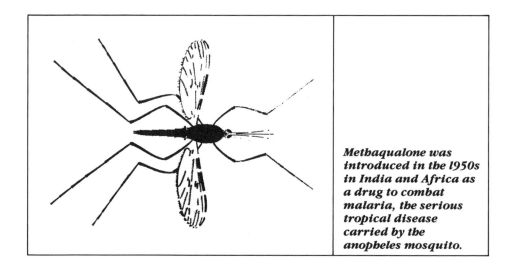

Methaqualone was introduced in the 1950s in India and Africa as a drug to combat malaria, the serious tropical disease carried by the anopheles mosquito.

conditions, fatal overdoses occasionally occur. In addition, unlike heroin, there is no antidote or drug that will reverse the effects of barbiturates if too much has been taken.

Because of these dangers and side effects, during the 1960s drug companies continued to search for a safe alternative to barbiturates. The first nonbarbiturate class of anesthetic agents, the eugenols, was introduced in 1963–1964, and the benzodiazepine group of tranquilizers (e.g., diazepam, or Valium) was introduced in 1963. However, these were not ideal anesthetic agents in terms of their safety and their ability to produce total muscle relaxation.

When in the 1970s methaqualone was tested as an anesthetic during surgery, it was thought to have many advantages over barbiturates and nonbarbiturate sedative/hypnotics. It was thought to have a wider margin of safety than the other drugs, and it produced excellent muscle relaxation with little effect on respiration. These studies were of a preliminary nature and more research was needed before methaqualone could be regularly used for anesthesia. However, because the negative reports about methaqualone began to increase in number, this research was never completed.

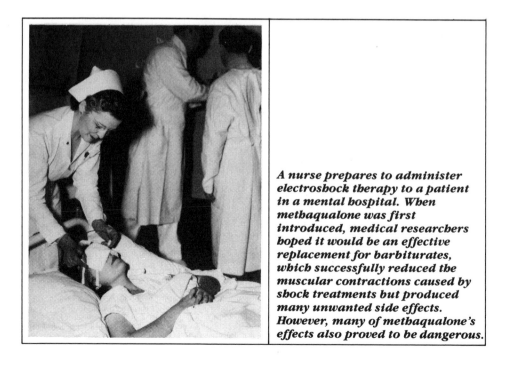

A nurse prepares to administer electroshock therapy to a patient in a mental hospital. When methaqualone was first introduced, medical researchers hoped it would be an effective replacement for barbiturates, which successfully reduced the muscular contractions caused by shock treatments but produced many unwanted side effects. However, many of methaqualone's effects also proved to be dangerous.

At the same time that medical uses of methaqualone became more doubtful, recreational use began to soar. Because methaqualone was not subject to government control and was thus easier to obtain than the other sedative/ hypnotics, it began to rise in popularity as a street drug. By 1972 it was one of the most popular drugs of abuse in the United States and was known as love drug, heroin for lovers, Dr. Jekyll and Mr. Hyde, sopors, sopes, ludes, mandrakes, and quacks. However, many reports began to surface about toxic reactions from taking too much methaqualone, and there were a large number of overdose cases arriving at hospital emergency rooms. Many regular users were becoming psychologically and physically dependent on methaqualone, and increasing numbers of people were seeking treatment for drug dependency at hospitals and clinics.

Regular users who attempted to stop taking methaqualone suffered severe withdrawal sickness, and some died from convulsions, coma, and respiratory failure. A common and dangerous practice of the drug user was to combine methaqualone with alcohol, a practice known as "luding out." When combined, these drugs produced many more adverse effects than either drug alone.

This appearance of methaqualone as an abused drug led the U.S. Senate to hold hearings in 1973 regarding the legal status of methaqualone. As a result of these hearings, in October 1973, methaqualone was classified as a Schedule II drug. A Schedule II drug is one which has a high rate of abuse, has the potential to produce dependence, and has an

While many experts consider infrequent use of methaqualone no more harmful than a rare alcoholic binge, they stress that most people find it extremely difficult to exercise moderation with such substances.

accepted medical use. It not only requires a prescription, but the physician has additional controls placed on him or her before prescribing the drug. A Schedule II drug is more difficult to obtain because its sales are recorded and manufacture is limited by quotas that are based partly on the previous year's sales. This classification made it more difficult for a drug abuser to obtain methaqualone, forcing some individuals to develop quasi-legal and illegal means of obtaining the drug.

One legal way of obtaining methaqualone appeared in the late 1970s and early 1980s, when stress clinics began to surface in Florida. These clinics were staffed by physicians and counselors who performed evaluations on individuals

Two phenomena that characterized the so-called Quaalude Culture of the 1970s were stress clinics, and juice bars, where methaqualone users assembled to "lude out" as they consumed fruit juice and danced to disco music.

who were allegedly experiencing severe stress. A typical visit included answering a short medical questionnaire administered by a counselor, and undergoing a brief physical examination. Afterwards the physician generally wrote a prescription for a month's supply of 300-mg (milligram) Quaalude tablets, which could be legally filled at any pharmacy. The cost of the clinic visit was $75 to $100, but because at that time the street price per tablet was approximately $5 to $7, significantly higher than the prescription price, an individual could sell some of the tablets on the street and, even after paying for the clinic visit, be left with a profit.

The increased evidence of methaqualone use and abuse as a result of these stress clinics led the Florida state legislature to ban Quaalude sales in 1982 by reclassifying methaqualone as a Schedule I drug. Schedule I drugs have no accepted medical use in the United States, and thus it is illegal to write a prescription for them. However, methaqualone remained a Schedule II drug in other states.

A DEA agent slices into a kilo bag of cocaine, part of the drug cache netted in a 1982 raid in Florida. Drug dealers often handle both cocaine and methaqualone which are shipped from Colombia, through Panama, and into the United States.

Although "bootleg" methaqualone (methaqualone manufactured in illegal labs) had been available since the early 1970s, Florida's reclassification of the drug increased the demand for and production of bootleg methaqualone. Bootleg methaqualone has been traced to tablet-pressing operations in Colombia. From there it is smuggled through the same channels as marijuana and cocaine, usually first appearing in the United States in Miami.

The widespread use of bootleg methaqualone introduced a new problem. What users thought were methaqualone tablets often turned out to be other drugs. A number of laboratories analyzed a quantity of bootleg methaqualone tablets and the published results showed that only 52% actually contained that drug.

Samples not containing methaqualone had one or more of the following: antihistamines (normally used to control allergic reactions), analgesics (painkillers), anesthetics (which cause a loss of sensation or consciousness and are used during surgery), barbiturates (sedative/hypnotics), antianxiety drugs, decongestants, diuretics, and fillers (substances, such as sugar, which are nontoxic). When a regular user's

Narcotic-squad vehicles converge on a DC-4 airplane whose pilot had tried to land unobserved near Baton Rouge, Louisiana. The plane's cargo included several million illegally produced Quaalude tablets.

supply of methaqualone no longer contains methaqualone there is always the danger that the user will suffer severe withdrawal sickness and even death from sudden abstinence.

In addition, many of the adulterants (or contaminants) can cause adverse side effects. Valium frequently appears in samples of bootleg methaqualone and if taken in high doses can result in serious problems, such as incoordination, nausea, vomiting, lethargy, and extreme fatigue. Another adulterant, phenobarbital (a barbiturate), is slower to take effect than is methaqualone and may lead users to take a large number of tablets to obtain an effect, thus increasing the risk of overdose and adverse reactions. As with methaqualone, if Valium and phenobarbital are taken in high doses for prolonged periods and then discontinued, the user may experience withdrawal symptoms.

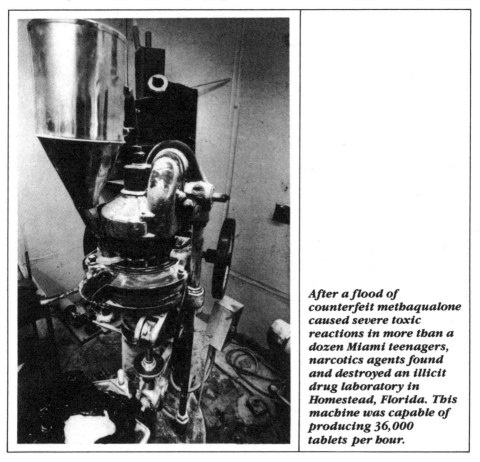

After a flood of counterfeit methaqualone caused severe toxic reactions in more than a dozen Miami teenagers, narcotics agents found and destroyed an illicit drug laboratory in Homestead, Florida. This machine was capable of producing 36,000 tablets per hour.

Bootleg methaqualone has also been found to contain orthotoludine, a compound present during the manufacture of methaqualone. Individuals ingesting bootleg methaqualone containing orthotoludine have experienced *necrotizing cystitis,* a serious condition which affects the bladder. Characterized by nausea, vomiting, and frequent, painful, and bloody urination, it requires prompt medical attention. Another contaminant in bootleg methaqualone has been identified as methylenedianaline, a substance which damages the liver.

As a result of the problems that arose from continued methaqualone abuse, in June 1984, following Florida's lead, the U.S. Congress reclassified methaqualone as a Schedule I substance. This became its nationally recognized classification. This reclassification occurred after Colombia, West Germany, Austria, Hungary, China, Switzerland, and India all virtually banned the drug between the years 1981 and 1983.

The Lemmon Company, the last U.S. manufacturer of methaqualone, stopped making the drug about a year before the ban and destroyed its stockpile. Though the company reported that it had stopped producing methaqualone be-

Employees of the sheriff's office in Broward County, Florida, examine tools that had been used to counterfeit the name of a drug company on illegal methaqualone tablets.

cause it realized the drug was being abused, profits did influence the company's decision—prescriptions for methaqualone were declining. Four million prescriptions were written in 1973 and only 300,000 in 1982—a 90% decline.

In spite of these actions, large quantities of methaqualone were still being seized by the Drug Enforcement Agency (DEA). In 1981 the DEA seized 57,173 kilograms, enough to make approximately 200 million tablets. However, by 1983 the number of kilograms seized had dropped to 1,000. In August 1984, 57 people were indicted in Miami for involvement in trafficking methaqualone. Operation Hammerhead resulted in the breakup of an international gang that allegedly handled 54 tons of methaqualone between 1981 and 1984.

Officials of the DEA attribute the success of this operation to the coordination of regulatory agency actions, legislation, and diplomatic initiatives at an international level. The U.S. attorney's office in Miami predicted, "You simply will not see illicit, counterfeit Quaalude tablets on the street any longer." According to the DEA this signaled the end of methaqualone use in this country. Only time would tell if methaqualone would disappear from the streets.

Classification and Chemistry

Methaqualone, 2-methyl-3-0-tolyl-4(3H)-quinazolinone, is one of the most potent of a series of sedative/hypnotic compounds ever marketed. Though not a barbiturate, it is structurally and functionally related to glutethimide, methyprylon,

Despite methaqualone's classification as a Schedule I substance, ads such as these frequently appear in drug-culture magazines.

and the barbiturates. In addition to having sedative/hypnotic properties, methaqualone also has anticonvulsant, antispasmodic, local anesthetic, and weak antihistaminic properties.

Methaqualone occurs as a white, bitter-tasting, crystalline powder, which can be taken orally in tablet or capsule form. Though methaqualone is soluble in alcohol and ether and slightly soluble in water, tests using intravenous preparations for the purpose of producing anesthesia were never completed to determine if intravenous administration is warranted.

The tablets, when produced by legal manufacturers, contained either 150 mg or 300 mg of methaqualone, and the capsules contained either 200 mg or 400 mg of methaqualone. However, bootleg methaqualone, produced in illegal and poorly controlled labs, contains varying amounts of methaqualone in addition to potentially hazardous adulterants.

An article in **High Times** *magazine, satirizing the illicit drug world, reported that "Quaalude botany and cultivation is intricate," and that "many working hours are required to bring up a superior Quaalude crop."*

In the 1970s discos such as New York City's Studio 54 were packed to capacity. The disco boom coincided with the sudden popularity of methaqualone, widely heralded as a safe way to enjoy a "boozeless drunk."

CHAPTER 2

THE SHORT-TERM EFFECTS OF METHAQUALONE

Methaqualone is a central nervous system depressant similar to the barbiturates. When taken in moderate doses (150 mg–300 mg) the drug produces a depression of brain function and a quiet, deep sleep. Higher doses (more than 300 mg) have been known to cause general anesthesia, depression, and seizures. Street users of methaqualone have reported a feeling of quiescence, relaxation, friendliness, and receptiveness, and a loss of inhibitions. These feelings led to methaqualone's reputation as an aphrodisiac, a drug that increases sexual desire. However, the notion that methaqualone enhances sexual performance and pleasure is not based on fact. Although methaqualone may lower inhibitions and increase sexual desire, it actually reduces an individual's ability to perform sexually.

Street users often combine methaqualone and alcohol (known as luding out). This combination produces a pleasant sense of well-being, an increased pain threshold, an impairment of proprioceptive (position) sense (which induces severe ataxia, or incoordination), and paresthesia, or a tingling of the fingers, lips, and tongue. The painless, pleasant ataxia frequently gives the user illusions of indestructibility,

Table 1

Short-Term Behavioral Effects of Methaqualone		
LOW DOSE (75 mg)	MODERATE DOSE (150 mg–300 mg)	HIGH DOSE (over 300 mg)
Calmness Relaxation Dizziness Tingling Numbness of extremities Drowsiness Restlessness Anxiety Burning	Euphoria Increased sociability Tingling or numbness throughout the body Self confidence Sexual arousal	General numbness Weakness Fear of "losing one's mind" Incoordination Agitation Panic

SOURCE: Addiction Research Foundation, Canada

which in turn may lead to euphoria. However, this state can be dangerous. There have been cases of users in this ataxic, euphoric state falling down a flight of stairs and not feeling the bruises until the following day. It would seem that the stupor produced by luding out would make sex almost impossible.

Some street users describe the methaqualone sensation as peaceful and calm, as a rush, or as similar to being drunk. Others actually claim that it is fighting off the urge to sleep which gives them a methaqualone high.

Table 1, taken from data collected by the Addiction Research Foundation in Canada, summarizes the short-term behavioral effects experienced by nonregular or nontolerant methaqualone users at different dosages.

The behavioral effects of methaqualone have been compared to those produced by other drugs. The University of Michigan's Institute for Social Research asked 17,700 high school seniors who reported using a psychoactive drug how long they stay high and how high they usually get on that drug. Not all seniors surveyed had used each of the drugs listed, nor could the dose of each drug be verified. The results are illustrated in Figure 1 and Figure 2.

The results of this questionnaire show that the high produced by methaqualone was not as intense as that produced by LSD and other psychedelics, but was more intense than the high reported for the other drugs. (Heroin was not included because the questions were not asked of the small number of heroin users; but averages from previous years indicated that heroin rankings would have been very similar to those of LSD.)

Figure 2 shows the perceived length of high from each drug. When studied in conjunction with Figure 1, one can conclude that those drugs that most often produce the greatest highs most frequently are the ones that last longest.

An analysis of trends over the years has indicated that since 1980 the degree and duration of the highs achieved by barbiturate users and methaqualone users are declining. The largest change has been in the duration of methaqualone highs, which has declined sharply in the last three or four years.

Moderate doses of methaqualone depress brain function and produce a deep sleep. Street users often report feeling relaxed, friendly, and uninhibited, effects which led to its reputation as an aphrodisiac.

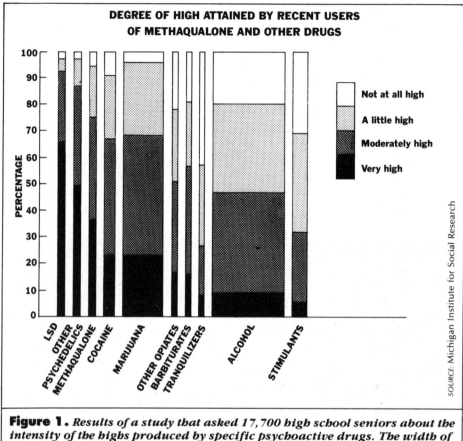

Figure 1. *Results of a study that asked 17,700 high school seniors about the intensity of the highs produced by specific psychoactive drugs. The width of each bar represents the number of seniors reporting any use of each drug over the previous 12 months.*

In addition to the psychoactive effects, methaqualone produces a number of undesirable side effects. These include headaches, dizziness, fatigue, and "hangovers" (here defined as continued sleepiness upon awakening). Some patients who have taken methaqualone to induce sleep have reported paresthesia (tingling) of the extremities prior to falling asleep. Also, patients have reported restlessness, anxiety, loss of appetite, nausea, vomiting, stomach discomfort, diarrhea, constipation, dry mouth, and cracking at the corners of the mouth. Nosebleeds and disturbances of the menstrual cycle have also been reported, as well as skin rash, itching, flushing, and increased sweating.

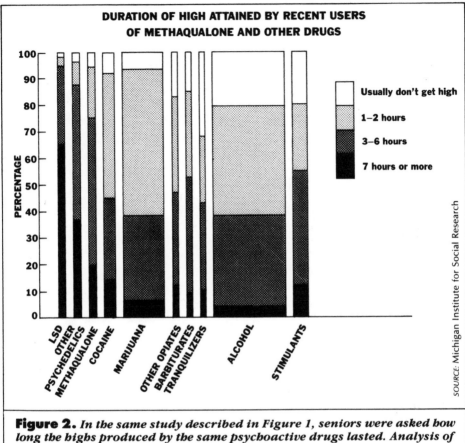

Figure 2. *In the same study described in Figure 1, seniors were asked how long the highs produced by the same psychoactive drugs lasted. Analysis of this study showed that the drugs that produced the most intense highs also had the most long-lasting effects.*

When the Drug Wears Off

When methaqualone is used to induce sleep, upon awakening the user may experience a hangover. The short-term user who takes methaqualone to induce sleep may also suffer a rebound effect when drug use ceases. When this occurs the user has sleeping difficulties even greater than those experienced before taking the drug.

For those who use methaqualone in high doses for a long time, the consequences of terminating drug use is much more severe. Sudden discontinuation may lead to severe withdrawal symptoms, such as nausea, vomiting, ner-

Table 2

	% EXPECTING	% EXPERIENCING
EFFECTS†	EFFECT	EFFECT
Relaxed feeling	95	100
Makes everything feel good	59	95
Escape from pressures	50	77
Lighthearted or high	68	93
Easy feeling, like to rap (talk)	73	87
To feel more confident	32	70
Get a drunk-like feeling without getting sick	53	80
Increase sensory sensations	30	59
Increases perception	5	17
Want to make love	77	97
To increase your sexual desires or break down sexual resistance of others	42	95
Desire to engage in physical activity	14	55
Numbness of the body	39	89
Tingling of the body	38	75
To feel more alert	2	15

Expected and Experienced Desirable Effects Associated with Methaqualone Use*

*Values are expressed as a percentage of those answering the question.
†Effects are expressed in street terms, as they appeared on the questionnaire.
SOURCE: Drs. Gerald and Schwirian

vousness, shakes, headache, anxiety, confusion, weakness, cramps, nightmares, insomnia, hallucinations, seizures, and even death. These symptoms resemble the withdrawal experienced by barbiturate users.

The Effect of Methaqualone on Behavior

During 1973 and 1974 a study was conducted on the behavior of 66 methaqualone users. They were primarily single, aged 22 to 25, and white. Of these users, 52% were college students; 55% were men, 42% were women, and 3% did not state their sex. Frequency of methaqualone use ranged from only a few times (39%) to monthly (28%) to several times daily (33%). Table 2 presents the expected and experienced desirable effects of methaqualone use reported.

In addition to describing the effects of methaqualone, the respondents were asked to rate their personalities. The results are shown in Table 3 and Table 4. The respondents were read several statements, each one describing a specific

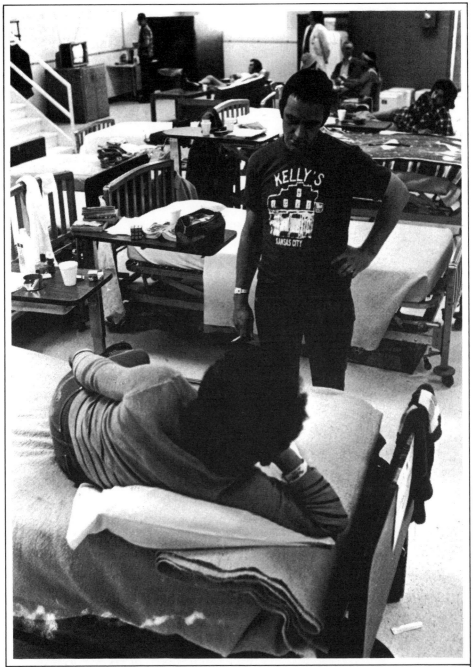

Experimental subjects at a research center in Kansas City. Researchers frequently use volunteers to test drugs never before used on humans.

Table 3

Self-Described Personality Scale Scores by Frequency of Methaqualone Use		
PERSONALITY CHARACTERISTIC	METHAQUALONE USE GROUP	USE GROUP AVERAGE*
Introverted	Daily Weekly Monthly	2.50 2.91 2.90
Extroverted	Daily Weekly Monthly	5.00 6.36 6.64
Depressed	Daily Weekly Monthly	3.05 3.73 3.27

*Scores range from 0 to 10, in which 0 = "seldom or never" and 10 = "most of the time." See text for explanation of terms and experimental design.
SOURCE: Drs. Gerald and Schwirian

Table 4

Self-Described Personality Scale Scores by Duration of Methaqualone Use		
PERSONALITY CHARACTERISTIC	METHAQUALONE USE GROUP (by duration)	USE GROUP AVERAGE*
Introverted	More than 1 year 6 months – 1 year Less than 6 months	2.40 2.86 2.96
Extroverted	More than 1 year 6 months – 1 year Less than 6 months	5.00 6.29 6.63
Depressed	More than 1 year 6 months – 1 year Less than 6 months	3.08 3.87 3.25

*Scores range from 0 to 10, in which 0 = "seldom or never" and 10 = "most of the time." See text for explanation of terms and experimental design.
SOURCE: Drs. Gerald and Schwirian

personality characteristic—introverted (inward-oriented), extroverted (outward-oriented), and depressed. For each statement, they were asked whether the description pertained to them "most of the time," "half of the time," or "seldom or never," and their answers were given scores of 10, 5, and 0, respectively. The researchers then categorized the ratings according to frequency and duration of methaqualone use.

These results of the study show that neither frequency nor duration of methaqualone use was significantly related to the respondents' self-described personality characteristics. However, those respondents most involved with methaqualone use rated themselves as being the least introverted, extroverted, and depressed.

These results should be interpreted with caution, however, because the sample size is small, there is no control group, and the ratings are self-reported rather than the opinions of mental health professionals. Also, drug actions vary greatly from one individual to another. What may be true for one individual using a drug may be entirely different for another individual using the same drug. See Appendix 1 for users' descriptions of the effect of methaqualone on their behavior.

People's self-descriptions do not always match the way others see them. Author Truman Capote, for example, drew himself (inset) as a bland, professorial individual, but to the public, he was a brilliant eccentric whose alcohol- and drug-inspired exploits often made headlines.

Table 5

Physiological Effects of Methaqualone in Short-Term, Nontolerant Users		
LOW DOSE (75 mg)	MODERATE DOSE (150–300 mg)	HIGH DOSE (more than 300 mg)
Drowsiness; sleep Fatigue Restlessness Headache Perspiration Dry mouth Loss of appetite Nausea; vomiting Stomach discomfort Diarrhea	More intense low-dose effects	Sleep Tremors Muscle spasms Profuse perspiration Rapid heart rate Motor incoordination Slurred speech Amnesia Chills Respiratory depression

SOURCE: Addiction Research Foundation, Canada

The Effect of Methaqualone on the Body

When taken orally methaqualone is absorbed by the stomach and intestine and widely distributed throughout the body, especially in fatty tissue. It has been detected in the liver, kidneys, heart, brain, spleen, cerebral spinal fluid, and skeletal muscles. The onset of action occurs within 30 minutes, and with doses of 150 mg to 300 mg sleep usually lasts 5 to 8 hours. As with methaqualone's subjective effects, the physiological effects are dependent upon the size of the dose. Table 5 summarizes the effects of methaqualone on the body for low, moderate, and high doses.

These effects usually disappear after 6 to 8 hours, although some effects may last 24 hours or longer. The respiratory depression produced by high doses of methaqualone is not as great as that produced by the barbiturates and other sedative/hypnotics.

The elimination of methaqualone from the body occurs in two phases. During the first, or distribution, phase the drug is distributed to the various parts of the body via the bloodstream. This process has a half-life of one to four hours, which means that half of the methaqualone will be distributed within this time period, half of the remaining half will be distributed within the subsequent period, and so on.

During the second, or elimination, phase the drug is removed from the body through metabolism and excretion.

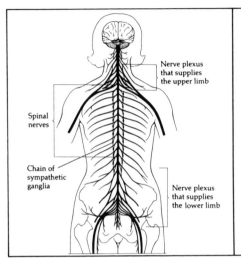

Figure 3. *Methaqualone acts on a different central-nervous-system site than other hypnotics, such as barbiturates. Once absorbed from the gastrointestinal tract it travels to the brain, where the drug reduces the intensity of the signals in the nerves. It is this effect which gives methaqualone its characteristic sleep-inducing and sedative quality.*

Nerve plexus that supplies the upper limb

Spinal nerves

Chain of sympathetic ganglia

Nerve plexus that supplies the lower limb

This phase's half-life, between 16 and 40 hours, represents the amount of time required for the body to remove half of a given dose. It takes about 5 half-lives to eliminate 99% of a given dose. The exact process of methaqualone metabolism is not completely understood. There is evidence that, when taken in therapeutic doses, methaqualone is almost completely metabolized by the liver. The inactive metabolites (the products of the drug's metabolism) are then excreted in the urine, bile, and feces. Less than 2% of a dose of methaqualone is excreted unchanged in the urine.

In addition to the side effects mentioned previously, methaqualone has been implicated in two cases of blood disorders and one case of mild seizures. Several individuals have experienced necrotizing cystitis, a bladder condition which results in painful and bloody urination. However, further investigation revealed that these individuals had ingested street methaqualone which had been contaminated with orthotoludine. Other street methaqualone samples have been found to contain methylenedianaline, a substance toxic to the liver.

The Risks Involved in Taking Methaqualone

While the specific risks involved with methaqualone abuse—such as behavioral toxicity, the development of tolerance and physical dependence, overdose, and death—will be discussed fully in Chapter 3, the more general risks associated with taking any drug will be considered here.

Even if a person is taking a drug for therapeutic benefit and as directed (following the prescribed schedule and dosage), there are still two major risks. Firstly, there is the risk of developing an abusive pattern. Secondly, there is the major risk of taking a substance that has not been sufficiently tested. All drugs must be tested according to FDA (Food and Drug Administration) guidelines before they are approved for public use, but unfortunately the testing is not as thorough before being released for sale by a drug company as they are afterwards. It is not unusual for a new drug to be introduced into the market with the high expectations that it is unique, superior to existing drugs, and not subject to abuse.

Methaqualone is an excellent example of a drug that initially appeared to be as effective as and much safer than preexisting alternatives, such as the barbiturates (see Figure 3). But that image of a safe methaqualone changed drastically after it had been widely prescribed and the side effects noted. Only then did manufacture of the drug stop, but after many lives had been damaged or lost in the interim. Tragically, there are a number of other drugs whose history has followed the same path as methaqualone's. Why does this happen?

In theory, as mentioned before, every new drug must go through rigorous clinical trials (tests in humans) before it is allowed on the U.S. market. These tests usually involve a large number of patients who volunteer to be "guinea pigs," ingesting a potentially hazardous and relatively unknown drug while being observed by investigators. The desired effects and any unusual reactions to the drug are noted, and the results are then reviewed by the FDA. However, these tests never involve the same number of patients who will use the drug once it is available on the market. Often, when a drug is finally released, because of the drug companies' and the doctors' enthusiasm, it is immediately prescribed to a very large number of patients and in many different situations. Essentially, it is only during this time that the true safety and effectiveness of the drug can be identified.

Methaqualone was introduced into the market at a time when certain portions of society were becoming involved with increased drug use and abuse. Unfortunately, the development of this drug-oriented subculture contributed to methaqualone becoming a highly abused substance. Some members of the drug subculture tried methaqualone because of its desirable sedative/hypnotic effects, and this, along with its low cost and high availability, contributed to the rapid growth of the drug's popularity and abuse.

An additional contributing factor to methaqualone's high abuse rate was the clinical tests' failure to identify the drug's abuse potential. Drug abuse, other than heroin addiction and alcoholism, had not yet been recognized as a large problem in our society. Because of this failure, access to methaqualone was not adequately controlled when it entered the market. It is surprising that there was a span of over 10 years between the time methaqualone abuse surfaced (1972) and its ban on a national level (1984).

The Results of Laboratory Studies

The effects of methaqualone and the symptoms which follow termination of its use have been studied by observing people who have taken the drug and have been in therapy or have been admitted to hospital emergency rooms. Heavy users have reported tolerance, physical dependence, and a general inability to function normally in society. However,

A protest against DES, a drug prescribed to prevent miscarriages but which also causes birth defects. DES was later withdrawn from the market, but remains a good example of an inadequately tested drug.

methaqualone users are often users of alcohol and/or other drugs, and thus it is often difficult to attribute these reported effects to methaqualone alone.

Laboratory studies on both humans and animals provide an even clearer picture of a drug's effects. Such controlled clinical experiments typically use volunteers who have entered a drug treatment program. The patients are usually informed about the drugs they will be receiving and told that they may also be given a placebo (a pill or capsule containing harmless substances that are not pharmacologically active). The placebo serves as a control with which the drug being tested can be compared under otherwise identical conditions. The drug samples and placebo are coded so that neither the experimenter nor the subject knows what is being administered until the end of the experiment.

One study was conducted to compare the abuse potential of methaqualone and other sedative/hypnotics. The 24 subjects, who were users of sedative/hypnotics, were given six treatments in random order, at one-week intervals. The six treatments consisted of a placebo, a 300-mg dose of methaqualone, and high and low doses of two nonbarbiturate sedative/hypnotics: diazepam (commonly known as Valium; 10 mg and 20 mg) and buspirone (10 mg and 40 mg). Before the treatment, and every hour for four hours afterward, the volunteers were tested to measure their moods.

The six treatments were evaluated on four scales that measured reactions to the drugs. On the stimulation scale methaqualone rated higher than all the other treatments, followed by the placebo and then the other two drugs. On

A teenager's first exposure to drugs very often occurs within the context of a group of friends, where peer pressure and the need to be accepted are strong.

the euphoria scale methaqualone again rated highest, followed by diazepam, buspirone, and placebo. Buspirone was rated highest on the unpleasantness scale. And on the abuse potential scale, estimated by whether or not the volunteer said he or she would use the drug again, the 20-mg dose of diazepam rated highest, followed by methaqualone, placebo, and, finally, buspirone.

The volunteers, using a 16-point scale in which 0 is "never," 8 "maybe," and 16 "definitely," were asked to report if they would ever take the drugs again. Only methaqualone (averaging 13.5) and the 20-mg dose of diazepam (10.6) exceeded the rating of "maybe." To determine the volunteers' assessment of overall worth, they were also asked to estimate the monetary street value of each treatment. Methaqualone ($3.50) and the 20-mg dose of diazepam ($1.94) were rated much higher than buspirone ($0.24) and the placebo ($0.23).

In another study, two doses of methaqualone (200 mg and 400 mg) were compared to a stimulant, d-amphetamine (15 mg and 30 mg), and two benzodiazepines, diazepam (10 mg) and prazepam (20 mg). Methaqualone was rated

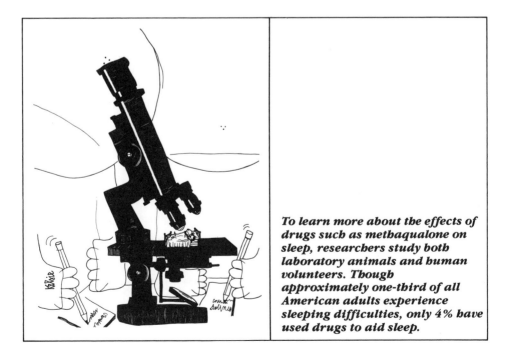

To learn more about the effects of drugs such as methaqualone on sleep, researchers study both laboratory animals and human volunteers. Though approximately one-third of all American adults experience sleeping difficulties, only 4% have used drugs to aid sleep.

high on stimulant and euphoriant effects, though the 10-mg dose of diazepam was reported as only slightly euphoric.

The few laboratory studies that have been conducted with human volunteers were concerned with the effects of methaqualone on complex learning processes and sleep. The delayed effects of the drug were also tested to determine whether small quantities of drug remaining in the body affected behavior.

In a 1980 Czechoslovakian study 19-year-old college students were tested on a learning task that required the student to learn specific associations between a number of tactile, aural, and visual stimuli presented by the experimenter. The students were tested before ingesting the drug and then again one and two hours after taking 300 mg of methaqualone. Results showed that methaqualone substantially increased the number of repetitions required for learning and decreased the number of correct responses.

Another experiment examined the effects of various sedative/hypnotics and their interaction with alcohol on tests of driving-related motor skills and coordination. A group of 40 volunteers was given amylobarbital, flurazepam, 250-mg methaqualone (combined with diphenhydramine, an antihistamine added to increase methaqualone's sedative effects), glutethimide, or placebo. The drugs or placebo were administered between 10 p.m. and 11 p.m. every night, and testing was conducted on the 7th and 14th mornings to determine whether there were any hangover effects on performance. The drugs were also tested when alcohol was given immediately before the test session. The subjects were tested for reaction time, coordination, and attention, and were asked to rate their own performance and the sedative/hypnotic effects of each substance.

Methaqualone (plus diphenhydramine) and flurazepam were rated as the strongest sedative/hypnotics. Methaqualone and glutethimide had no hangover effect on performance, but amylobarbital and flurazepam impaired eye-hand coordination, an effect exaggerated by the addition of alcohol.

In a later study a higher dose of methaqualone (500 mg) was used, and it was found that alcohol did increase the persistent effects of methaqualone on performance. Twelve volunteers were given methaqualone (or placebo) at 10:30 p.m. On the next three days at 5:30 p.m. they were given

500 mg of alcohol (or placebo) in a lemon-flavored drink. On the day before drinking alcohol and 20 minutes after drinking it they were given a series of tests. The first measured their mood states and level of arousal; the second measured visual activity; and the third was a sensitive measure of mental processing.

When the subjects received alcohol 24 hours after taking methaqualone they felt slower mentally and significantly more drowsy, lethargic, and incompetent than when they received alcohol after taking placebo tablets. Performance on the visual acuity test and the test of mental processing was affected more by the combination of methaqualone and alcohol treatments then by either drug alone.

As a sedative/hypnotic, the primary effects of methaqualone are the induction of sleep and sedation. And thus, laboratory research has been directed toward the drug's effectiveness in producing these effects. One of the first questions to be addressed was, "Does methaqualone produce normal sleep?" It was already known that patients who have been prescribed methaqualone generally sleep for 6 to 8 hours after taking the drug, and so researchers were interested in whether or not this sleep was like normal sleep, and whether or not sleep was affected after the person stopped taking the drug.

Sleep time can be measured by observing an individual in a sleep laboratory and/or by accepting his or her self-report. In the sleep laboratory the physiological aspects of sleep are measured by a painless procedure that involves

Czechoslovakia was a major producer of methaqualone and a source for the black market, but under U.S. pressure it halted production in 1982.

placing electrodes on a person's head and recording the electrical activity of the brain. The record of electrical activity is called an electroencephalogram, or EEG.

During normal sleep there are two major stages, and these stages alternate. The first stage is called paradoxical, or rapid eye movement (REM), sleep, and it is during this stage that dreaming occurs. The other stage is called orthodox, or nonREM, sleep. This stage is further divided into four stages, during which muscles become progressively more relaxed, blood pressure, heart rate, and temperature decline, and breathing becomes slow and regular. During the fourth stage of nonREM sleep the person is most deeply asleep.

The EEG is characterized by slow waves and spindles (long, narrow spikes) during nonREM sleep, and by faster waves with no spindles during REM sleep. The EEG during REM sleep looks very much like it would when the person is awake, although it may be very difficult to wake a person during REM (thus the term paradoxical sleep). For normal, restful sleep it is necessary that both of these sleep stages occur. The percentage of time spent in REM sleep is relatively constant from night to night and across all age groups ranging from children to the elderly. A normal sleep cycle usually consists of 70 to 100 minutes of nonREM sleep before REM sleep begins. REM periods then occur about every 90 minutes, and they occupy about 20% to 25% of the total sleeping time.

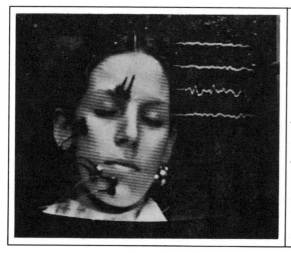

A participant in a sleep-lab experiment has her brain waves recorded. In an 8-hour period the sleep pattern of a normal young adult usually includes four separate periods of REM (rapid eye movement) sleep, during which a person dreams. Methaqualone suppresses REM sleep and thus reduces the number of dreams which can threaten mental stability.

Studies of the effects of methaqualone on normal sleep have produced mixed results. The pharmaceutical companies that initially tested the drug claimed that methaqualone produced only a minor suppression of REM sleep and no increase in REM sleep when a person stopped taking the drug. However, a series of studies by a group of independent researchers disputed these claims. They found that the usual dose of methaqualone (300 mg) produced a significant suppression in REM sleep, and that a pronounced increase, or rebound effect, occurred after the individual stopped taking the drug. These effects did not occur when a smaller amount was taken (150 mg).

Another study found similar effects of methaqualone on REM sleep, but found no rebound upon withdrawal. They concluded that 300 mg of methaqualone did not differ from comparable doses of the nonbarbiturate sedative/hypnotics, such as glutethimide (500 mg) and methyprylon (300 mg), and the barbiturates, such as secobarbital (100 mg) and pentobarbital (100 mg). Thus, it appears that methaqualone offered no advantages over the existing sleep medications.

Laboratory studies with animals have been primarily concerned with demonstrating *tolerance* and *physical dependence* to methaqualone. Tolerance is defined as a decrease in the effects of a drug compared to its initial actions, over a period of repeated administrations. Physical dependence is measured by a withdrawal sickness, which occurs when frequent use of a drug is abruptly terminated.

In one study with rats, tolerance was measured by comparing changes in body weight, body temperature, and spontaneous motor activity before and during a period when methaqualone was added to the daily diet. It was found that methaqualone lowered the temperature and decreased the activity level of the rats, but there was a gradual return to normal levels within 7 days. When, after the normal levels were regained, the drug dosage was then tripled, there was an initial decrease in temperature and activity, but normal levels again returned by the end of the second week. Finally, the amount of methaqualone was increased during the third week by over 100 mg/kg, and similar results occurred. There was also a decline in body weight accompanying the highest dose. At the end of the 21 days methaqualone was removed from the diet and the withdrawal syndrome was studied.

When presented with auditory stimuli, 60% of the rats developed convulsions on the second day. Food intake, body weight, temperature, and activity level were not affected by methaqualone withdrawal.

In this same study another group of rats was treated similarly, except that they received the barbiturate phenobarbital instead of methaqualone. These rats showed a similar, though less complete, development of tolerance. All of the rats in this group experienced seizures when the drug was removed. In addition, these rats stopped taking food, displayed a large drop in body weight, suffered from diarrhea, and had an increase in temperature and activity level. About 30% of the rats from the phenobarbital group died from the convulsions, while none in the methaqualone group did.

Although it is impossible to equate the doses to compare directly methaqualone and phenobarbital, these results suggest that the physical dependence produced by methaqualone occurs less frequently and is milder than that produced by phenobarbital.

A similar study of tolerance and physical dependence in rats compared those animals that received methaqualone to those that received the combination of methaqualone and the antihistamine diphenhydramine. The rats given methaqualone developed tolerance within one week; and when the amount of methaqualone was increased the second week they showed complete tolerance. However, the group receiving the methaqualone/diphenhydramine combination showed only incomplete tolerance by the end of the second week. This was confirmation that the drug combination had a greater depressant effect than methaqualone alone. When the drugs were no longer added to the food, 70% of the rats receiving methaqualone had convulsions by the second day, but none of the rats died. All of the rats receiving the drug combination suffered convulsions, and half of them died. The results also show that the addition of diphenhydramine to methaqualone produces a more severe withdrawal syndrome than methaqualone alone.

Tolerance and physical dependence were also produced in mice that had been exposed to methaqualone in their food pellets for 36 days. Tolerance was measured by the reduction in sleep time following an injection of methaqualone. Physical dependence was measured by recording how susceptible the mice were to convulsions produced by exposing the animals to a gas that affects the nervous system. Almost all animals will convulse after exposure to this gas, but those suffering from methaqualone withdrawal do so sooner. The mice were tested for withdrawal syndrome 18 hours after the drug had been removed from the food. Mice tested after longer intervals did not exhibit withdrawal symptoms, but more research is needed to determine whether 18 hours represents the peak effect.

Additional studies with methaqualone and laboratory animals have been concerned with physiological and behavioral effects. For instance, researchers found that 75 mg/kg of methaqualone caused incoordination and loss of the righting reflexes (which allow an animal to land on its feet) in rats and mice. When dogs were given 120 mg/kg they initially lost their coordination and became excitable. Later they vomited, urinated, and defecated. After 3 hours they were totally immobilized, and this paralysis lasted for more than 8 hours. They did not recover completely for 48 hours. Methaqualone did not have any effect on heart rate and did not produce pupil dilation.

The amount of methaqualone given to the dogs was equivalent to a 9,000-mg dose given to a person—30 times

"Boy, do we have this guy conditioned.
Every time I press the bar down he drops a pellet in."

the usual dose. However, it is difficult to compare amounts of drug taken across species because animals such as monkeys and dogs are often much less sensitive to drugs than people, and rodents (e.g., rats, mice) are even less sensitive than dogs and monkeys.

Other physiological changes attributed to methaqualone (based on animal studies) are alterations in processes that regulate body temperature and loss of response to sound or painful stimuli. Methaqualone also blocks tremors and convulsions, which can be experimentally induced by certain drugs, by electric shock, and by loud noise.

One study compared the effects of methaqualone, diazepam (Valium), and pentobarbital (another sedative/hypnotic) on three measures of behavior in rats. The first measure, referred to as conditioned suppression of drinking, involved a procedure whereby the rats were trained to drink from a tube for 10 minutes each day. Occasionally a tone was sounded for 7 seconds, during the last 5 seconds of which

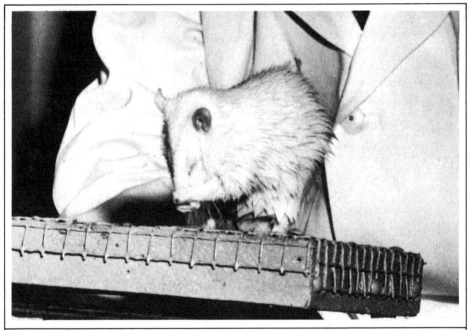

Extensive experiments with laboratory rats have contributed to researchers' understanding of methaqualone's physiological and behavioral effects, including tolerance and dependence.

the rats received a shock if they continued to drink. They typically did not drink during the shock, and conditioned suppression occurred when drinking stopped as soon as the tone was sounded.

The second task required the rats to walk on a rotating rod (called a rotarod) for at least 180 seconds. The third test measured their physical activity by automatically recording the amount they walked within an electromagnetic field.

All three drugs, in doses up to 6 to 10 times the smallest amount tested, increased the amount of drinking during shocks, i.e., decreased the conditioned suppression— the rats did not respond appropriately to the tone and therefore received shocks. Rotarod performance was significantly disrupted by 30 mg/kg diazepam and 19 mg/kg methaqualone, and all three drugs, each in doses of 18 mg/kg, significantly decreased motor activity. Pentobarbital had the largest effect and methaqualone the smallest.

In this study another drug, Ro 15-1788, was also administered—by itself and in combination with the other drugs. This drug is known to reverse, or antagonize, some effects of diazepam. In the experiment just described, Ro 15-1788 did indeed reverse the increase in shock punishment which was the result of diazepam, and did increase the punished drinking which had been induced by pentobarbital.

Ro 15-1788 reversed the disruption in rotarod performance produced by diazepam and increased the disruption due to pentobarbital. Decreased motor activity produced by diazepam was almost completely reversed by Ro 15-1788, but the decreases resulting from pentobarbital were unchanged. Ro 15-1788 had no effect on any of these measures when it was administered alone or in combination with methaqualone. These experiments indicate that while sedative/hypnotics may produce similar alterations in behavior, they probably act on different parts of the brain.

Finally, in a study of learning and memory, rats were trained to swim down a white- or black-painted alley in a maze that resembled the shape of the letter T. The rats were rewarded with food for choosing the white side, but were not rewarded for choosing the black side. Following the injection of 25 mg/kg–30 mg/kg methaqualone the animals made significantly more errors.

Some people take methaqualone to cure insomnia, while others resist its soporific (sleep-inducing) effects, preferring to stay awake to experience the relaxation and drowsy euphoria it produces.

CHAPTER 3

THE EFFECTS OF CHRONIC METHAQUALONE USE

*T*hose who begin to use methaqualone frequently soon experience tolerance. This is characterized by a need to increase the dosage to receive the same effect as previously experienced, or when less of an effect is experienced by a fixed dosage taken repeatedly over time. Tolerance and loss of tolerance are important considerations for those who frequently use drugs. For instance, though methaqualone users may increase the dosage by as much as ten times, they will gradually become tolerant to the sleep-producing effects. However, if the users stop taking methaqualone for a period of time, or switch to a different drug and then return to methaqualone, the large doses taken in the past may now cause overdose, coma, or death.

Tolerance to the sleep-producing effects of methaqualone develops rapidly, especially when the drug is used nightly for sleep. Tolerance also develops quickly to the "high," or euphoria, which is sought by daytime users. To maintain the drug's pleasurable effects users typically increase their dosage and the frequency of ingestion. Initially, methaqualone users may take a 75-mg tablet four times each day, or a total of 300 mg per day, to achieve mild sedative and euphoric effects. For a new user, 300 mg ingested at one time would produce sleep, but as tolerance develops to the sleep-producing effects, the user may need to take several 300-mg tablets, totaling 1,000 mg–2,000 mg per day. This represents a threefold to sevenfold increase in the amount of drug taken.

Individuals also vary considerably in their sensitivity to methaqualone, and in their ability to develop tolerance to

A federal drug agent displays capsules and equipment seized during a raid on a Pittsburgh methaqualone laboratory. This fully operational lab was capable of producing 50 pounds of the drug per day.

the drug. Some users have died from taking as little as 8,000 mg while others have taken as much as 22,000 mg and survived.

Another factor to consider is that there is cross-tolerance between methaqualone and other sedative/hypnotic drugs. This means that once users are tolerant to methaqualone they will also need greater amounts of other drugs to produce the effects they expect from those drugs. Similarly, once individuals are tolerant to other sedative/hypnotic drugs, they will need a larger amount (than nontolerant individuals) of methaqualone to obtain the desired effect.

There is another reason why developing tolerance to methaqualone can be dangerous. Though the amount of drug needed to get high rapidly increases in the frequent user, the amount of methaqualone that will result in death remains about the same regardless of how often the drug is used. Since the regular daily amount and the fatal amount become dangerously close, fatal overdoses become more likely for the tolerant user, especially when the user combines methaqualone and alcohol. A few drinks combined with a high methaqualone dose can result in coma and death.

With other psychoactive drugs, such as heroin and phencyclidine (PCP, or angel dust), the amount needed to kill a user increases as the person becomes tolerant, just as the amount needed to produce a "high" increases with regular use. Thus, the margin of safety, although it is often not large with some drugs, does not shrink as the person becomes tolerant.

This margin of safety is measured by what is called the therapeutic ratio. This ratio is the amount of drug needed to cause death divided by the amount of the drug needed to produce a minimal therapeutic effect. In a nontolerant user the therapeutic ratio for methaqualone is about 14.3, though this ratio decreases considerably, to as low as 2 or 3, as tolerance develops. For comparison, the therapeutic ratio of phenobarbital (a barbiturate used to provide sedation or sleep) is 10; however, this ratio remains fairly constant even as the person becomes tolerant. But in a tolerant methaqualone user the margin of safety is very small, and it would thus take only a small mistake or miscalculation to produce a fatal overdose.

Psychological Dependence

When a person begins to use methaqualone on a regular and repeated basis, he or she is showing evidence of *drug dependence*. Drug dependence exists when a drug serves as a reward for the behavior that leads to taking it. This definition makes it possible to measure drug dependence, such as by the number of times prescriptions are refilled or by the number of pills purchased in the illegal market. *Psychological dependence* has occurred when the drug user experiences a strong craving for a drug, and finds it impossible to stop taking it. However, this term is not easy to quantify and to define objectively.

Psychological dependence on methaqualone can exist when low doses are taken at irregular intervals, or even when the person is no longer taking the drug. Methaqualone users have discovered their psychological dependence in a

Their drinks close at hand, Las Vegas casino patrons prepare to place their bets. Individuals with addictive personalities frequently exhibit more than one type of habitual behavior, sometimes simultaneously. Compulsive gamblers, for example, are often also addicted to narcotics, tobacco, and/or alcohol.

number of ways. Often methaqualone was taken when barbiturate and other nonbarbiturate sedative/hypnotics were not available. Because methaqualone seemed to have more pleasurable effects and less undesirable effects, users reported difficulty switching back to the drugs they were accustomed to taking.

Other people discovered their dependence on methaqualone when they stopped taking the drug. They became ill and exhibited a number of withdrawal symptoms, described in the next section. Even after these symptoms had disappeared and individuals had not taken the drug for a long period, a craving for the drug still existed. These users were preoccupied with thoughts of the drug and with behavior that was associated with its previous use.

Another type of user may show psychological dependence on methaqualone when he or she has become tolerant to the desired effects of the drug, but does not increase the dosage or frequency of ingestion. Although the drug may no

longer produce any significant psychological effects, these users are resistant to discontinuing its use. They often experience anxiety or panic when they encounter difficulties obtaining the drug.

Physical Dependence

Physical dependence refers to a disruption in biological processes after a person abruptly stops taking a drug. Physical dependence often occurs along with drug dependence, but it is not a necessary condition for drug dependence.

A therapist in a trauma room attends to a young woman who took a drug overdose and went into a coma. Because methaqualone's margin of safety is very small, even a slight miscalculation can lead to overdose.

Table 6

Methaqualone Withdrawal Symptoms	
MILD	SEVERE
Restlessness Irritability; antisocial behavior Insomnia Headache Mild tremors Loss of appetite Nausea and vomiting Abdominal cramps Muscle twitches	Mental confusion Delirium Nightmares Hallucinations Bleeding from the stomach High fever* Epileptic-like seizures* *can be fatal

Unlike psychological dependence, physical dependence is easy to define and measure.

Physical dependence on methaqualone often results when a person regularly takes large doses of the drug. There are great differences among individuals in what constitutes a large dose, but it could be anything from 600 mg to 3,000 mg per day (two to ten 300-mg tablets) for a three- to four-week period. When methaqualone is abruptly withdrawn the initial withdrawal symptoms appear within one to three days, and may last for several days. A mild form of withdrawal, which occurs after stopping light to moderate use, includes the symptoms listed in Table 6.

More severe withdrawal results from termination of heavier methaqualone use. Symptoms may occur immediately and last for a week or more. The mild symptoms are intensified and the additional severe symptoms appear (see Table 6).

Untreated withdrawal from methaqualone and other sedative/hypnotics is more severe and more likely to result in death than withdrawal from drugs such as heroin. Careful observation and management in addition to the administration of nonbarbiturate sedative/hypnotics has been effective in controlling severe symptoms of methaqualone withdrawal. The severe withdrawal symptoms can be avoided if the heavy user seeks the help of a physician before terminating methaqualone use. Gradual detoxification is accomplished by decreasing the daily dose by 150 mg every one to three days. The patient may be hospitalized and a long-acting barbiturate substituted for methaqualone. Eventually the barbiturate, too, is gradually withdrawn.

Signs of Toxicity and Overdose

The dose-dependent effects of methaqualone in the long-term, tolerant, methaqualone user are similar to those reported in Chapter 2. However, in the long-term user there are also reliable signs of toxicity (poisoning). The high doses taken by frequent users result in long-term impairment of thought processes, altered muscular functions, visual disturbances, emotional instability, and sleep disorders such as insomnia. Some individuals experience a form of toxic psychosis characterized by delusions, hallucinations, disorientation, and confusion. This condition disappears within three to five days if the methaqualone intake is substantially

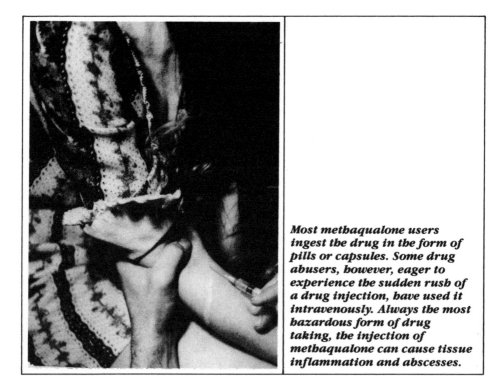

Most methaqualone users ingest the drug in the form of pills or capsules. Some drug abusers, however, eager to experience the sudden rush of a drug injection, have used it intravenously. Always the most hazardous form of drug taking, the injection of methaqualone can cause tissue inflammation and abscesses.

Table 7

Symptoms of Methaqualone Overdose
Vomiting Marked salivation Rapid changes in pupil size and reaction to light Respiratory depression Cardiovascular depression Decreased muscle tone Insensitivity to physical pain or loud noises Coma with extreme muscle rigidity (lasting 4 to 5 days)

reduced. More common signs of toxicity in a tolerant user is an unkempt, disheveled appearance and a generally fatigued look—signs also characteristic of regular users of other sedative/hypnotic drugs.

Overdose of and toxic reactions to methaqualone are much more likely to occur in regular users between the ages of 18 and 24. Because there are many repeated incidents of overdose among the same individuals, it is believed that those in this age group have either an inability or disinclination to regulate the amount they ingest.

Adverse reactions to methaqualone are also heavily dependent upon the source, availability, and quality of the illegally manufactured drug. Table 7 summarizes the symptoms that characterize methaqualone overdose. As the patient begins to recover from methaqualone overdose, depending on the severity and length of coma (if any), he or she may suffer complicating conditions, such as kidney failure, brain damage, gastrointestinal or retinal hemorrhage, and facial or pulmonary (lungs) edema (swelling).

Causes of Death

Death due to methaqualone overdose is caused by a failure of the lungs, kidneys, liver, and /or heart. Initially, an overdose produces muscle spasms, jerky movements, tension in the muscles, and restlessness. Then the patient becomes delirious, and convulsions, such as the grand mal seizures that occur with epilepsy, may set in. Coma often follows.

Unlike overdose with other sedative/hypnotics, such as the barbiturates, the person still has a gag reflex and thus can vomit. Complications can occur if, when a person vomits, fluid and food particles enter his or her breathing pathway. Inhalation of stomach contents may obstruct breathing and cause the lungs to excrete excessive amounts of fluids, making it extremely difficult to breathe.

Fluids may also accumulate in the blood vessels. Liver and kidney damage may result, and the heart rate and temperature may become abnormally high. Methaqualone overdose may also result in shock (a lowering of the heart rate and body temperature) or respiratory arrest, but the drug is less likely than the barbiturates to produce these results. Most deaths due to methaqualone overdose have occurred when the drug was combined with alcohol, resulting in respiratory failure.

A study of methaqualone-related deaths, published in 1983 and covering the period from 1971 to 1982 in Dade County (Miami), Florida, investigated 246 deaths in which methaqualone was found in the body fluids or tissues. More than three-fourths of the deaths occurred after 1977, and the number of deaths continued to rise through 1981. An

This scorpion-like creature was drawn by a young drug-clinic patient who said it was crawling on the floor of his room. Such frightening hallucinations, the result of a form of toxic psychosis which may accompany chronic, heavy use of methaqualone, usually disappear soon after drug use is discontinued.

interesting finding from this study was that since 1977, 72% of the methaqualone-related deaths were due to trauma that occurred while the person was under the influence of the drug. Only 17% were explained by drug overdose. The remaining 1% died of causes unrelated to methaqualone use.

Of the 68 overdose deaths in the Dade County study, 40 were accidental and 28 were suicidal. The comparatively high cost of bootleg methaqualone ($5 to $7 per tablet) and the fact that the bootleg product may not contain the expected 300 mg may contribute to the relatively low rate of death by overdose. Since 1979 the number of overdose deaths has been increasing. No deaths or physical abnormalities were attributed to long-term use of methaqualone.

Nearly 70% of the deaths were white males ranging in age from 13 to 70 years. An additional 26% of the deaths were white females; less than 5% of the people were black. The type of trauma that caused death was divided into vehicular accidents (33%), nonvehicular accidents (10%), traumatic suicides (16%), and murders (13%). In most of the vehicular accidents the methaqualone user was driving. Although alcohol was also detected in nearly 75% of these victims, the blood alcohol level of most of the people was too low for them to be considered legally intoxicated. However, the pre-crash behavior of these drivers was described by observers to be similar to that of a grossly intoxicated individual. Drowning and falling were the major causes of nonvehicular accidents.

In most instances in the study, the traumatic suicides involved the use of handguns, although hangings and drownings were also reported. The homicide victims were usually shot by the police or another person while committing a felony. No methaqualone users were responsible for the deaths of others, except for one pair of users whose deaths resulted from a suicidal "Russian roulette."

These findings indicate that, in terms of an individual's ability to function in the environment, the changes in behavior are a far more serious consequence of methaqualone use than overdose. The effects of methaqualone alone or in combination with alcohol—poor judgment, impulsive actions, and motor incoordination—are as likely to have traumatic results for the user as they are for drug-free members of the immediate environment.

Actress Susan Sarandon pops pills in a scene from the movie Joe, *which deals with a young drug user and her parents' reactions to her behavior. Unfortunately, most drug abusers do not seek treatment until they suffer from overdose or experience personal problems.*

CHAPTER 4

MEDICAL TREATMENT FOR METHAQUALONE ABUSE

Methaqualone, usually taken by mouth in tablet form, is absorbed by the gastrointestinal tract, metabolized in the liver, and excreted in the urine and feces. Sensitive laboratory tests can detect methaqualone in the body and measure the amount in body fluids. However, some of these tests are expensive and time-consuming, and often they require large amounts of blood or urine.

Both gas and thin-layer chromatography (a scientific technique which separates a solution into its parts, thus permitting measurement of each one) have been used to detect and quantify methaqualone in blood and urine; however, these delicate processes require more time than the duration of the overdose effects. Thus, diagnosis and treatment have to rely on an assessment of the patient's condition, and the laboratory test can only verify the diagnosis after the fact.

Furthermore, methaqualone blood levels are not always an accurate indicator of a patient's condition. An evaluation of these measurements must consider how frequently a person takes the drug and how much tolerance he or she has developed. A tolerant individual is able to withstand much higher concentrations of methaqualone than one who uses methaqualone infrequently. A level of 1.7 mg methaqualone per 100 ml of blood plasma produces a light level of unconsciousness in which the individual is still responsive to mild pain. However, as much as 9 mg/100 ml of plasma has been found to produce the same level of unconsciousness in tolerant individuals. Levels of 2.5 mg/100 ml–3 mg/100 ml of plasma are considered to be in the range of dangerous poisoning for nontolerant persons. The lethal dose of methaqualone is approximately 114 mg/kg–133 mg/kg of body weight.

Radioimmunoassay methods have been used to detect methaqualone and/or its metabolites (the products of the metabolism of methaqualone) in urine for at least five days after administration. This technique, relatively rapid and simple compared to chromatography, measures the interaction between a radioactive drug and the drug which is being measured. Because the radioactive drug will not react with any other abused drugs, radioimmunoassay is a sensitive measuring technique for methaqualone.

Detection of methaqualone in urine has been useful not only for confirming an overdose diagnosis but for preventing and treating drug abuse in military personnel. Legal and illegal methaqualone is readily available in European countries, and in the 1970s methaqualone use was high among American military forces stationed there. Beginning in September 1973 all military personnel were subject to a urinalysis. The test identified individuals who were using drugs, and once their use was revealed they more readily admitted

A Massachusetts Institute of Technology doctor prepares to test the blood of a patient who is the apparent victim of a methaqualone overdose. The blood sample will be injected into the lab's computerized organic analysis system, which can automatically determine which of several hundred drugs the patient might have ingested.

drug use. They cooperated by providing information on the extent of their use, and the sources and economics of the drug(s) they were using.

A follow-up study indicated that practically all personnel who were confirmed as drug abusers entered the army's drug rehabilitation program. Other studies have indicated that mass urinalysis also prevented drug use in many individuals. However, in July 1974, this practice was terminated due to legal action against the military. Forced urinalysis was judged illegal on the grounds that an individual cannot be forced to testify against him- or herself.

Treating Methaqualone Abuse

Unfortunately, the segment of the population that is most prone to drug abuse—adolescents and young adults—is also the group that is most resistant to treatment. Abusers of methaqualone and other sedatives do not seek treatment until overdose occurs or difficulties with family, school, job, or legal authorities arise. Hospitalization and detoxification is the first step. Later, drug therapy may be a part of the treatment, especially if an underlying psychosis or depression was the basis for the self-medication that led to compulsive drug use. Antipsychotics, antidepressants, lithium, and even small amounts of benzodiazepines (such as Valium, given for short periods of time) might be necessary for disturbed patients.

There are several treatment programs useful for methaqualone abusers. These include school-based programs; age-

A toxicologist checks the results of drug tests run on American soldiers in 1971. Due to legal action against the armed forces, their compulsory urinalysis program was discontinued in 1974, but other military antidrug efforts remain in operation.

oriented treatment facilities such as recreational and counseling centers; community groups such as boys' clubs or religious groups; therapeutic communities; and milieu therapy, which provides inpatient and outpatient therapeutic communities with extensive medical and psychiatric assistance.

Continued contact and follow-up are essential, and with younger clients home visits may be necessary. One of the important goals of any treatment program is to facilitate readmission to treatment if the patient fails to successfully detoxify and returns to drug abuse. In his book *Substance Abuse Disorders in Clinical Practice* Dr. Senay outlines general guidelines for treatment of substance abuse.

General Treatment Guidelines for Substance Abuse

1. The substance abuse should be treated as a primary disorder and not secondary to another problem.

2. First the patient must be informed about the structure of the treatment plan, that it consists of several elements and that it is long-term (often one to two years).

3. The patient should understand that change will have to occur in many aspects of life (e.g., family interactions, friends, attitudes, and environment).

4. It will be necessary to involve the family for support and as a source of information and family history for psychiatric assessment. Substance abusers have high rates of depressive disorders.

5. The patient will require frequent monitoring for general health measures such as diet and exercise, for the presence of drug in urine and blood, for side effects of therapeutic drugs (e.g., antidepressants), and to maintain regular contact with the therapist.

6. A recovering substance abuser should be exposed to models and later encouraged to serve as a role model for other patients. Education about the effects of the abused drugs and other drugs should be provided.

Treating Methaqualone Overdose

Treating methaqualone overdose consists primarily of intensive supportive therapy during the period when the peak drug effects are occurring and subsiding. Extreme measures to remove methaqualone from the blood, such as diuresis (inducing increased excretion of urine), can lead to heart failure; and dialysis (a method by which the blood is mechanically purified) has not been able to remove sufficient quantities of methaqualone from the blood. Suctioning of gastric contents (pumping the stomach) is difficult because the gag reflex may still be intact, and insertion of a stomach tube may produce choking, convulsions, or other adverse effects. Thus, the situation must be evaluated very carefully; each step of the treatment depends upon the response of the individual.

If the patient arrives at the emergency room in a conscious state, he or she is briefly questioned about the ingested drug, and vomiting is induced. Samples of vomitus, blood, or urine are taken for analysis of drug content. Further absorption of the drug by the gastrointestinal system can be prevented by administering charcoal and cathartics. To insure proper breathing, an open airway is established by inserting a tube into the trachea, and often it is necessary to administer oxygen to prevent brain damage from lack of oxygen. Pulse and blood pressure are monitored frequently.

When the patient's condition has stabilized, he or she is continuously observed, and changes in heart rate, respiration rate, and level of consciousness are noted by the staff.

Counselling programs, such as this one at Phoenix House in New York City, provide therapy to ex-drug users, often employing positive role models and drug education programs while offering patients a supportive environment after drug use is terminated.

When it is determined that the patient is fully conscious, a program of detoxification (gradual discontinuation of drug use) and psychiatric counseling may be set up, especially if the patient is a chronic drug user.

When a patient enters the emergency room in a semi-comatose or comatose state, his or her airway may be cleared, but often the patient cannot tolerate a tube being inserted to the stomach for suctioning gastric contents. Similarly it may be difficult to insert a tube to assist breathing. Dehydration is prevented by administering intravenous liquids. Heart and respiratory functioning are monitored, and assisted respiration is given if needed. Conservative management with good nursing care in the intensive care unit generally gives the best results. When the patient is fully conscious, he or she is referred to a detoxification unit and/or to psychiatric counseling.

The recreation room at Phoenix House provides a drug-free environment in which young people, separated from their past drug-oriented lives, can enjoy music and conversation and feel accepted by their peers.

Detoxification from methaqualone should be conducted in a hospital setting. There are two major ways of detoxifying the methaqualone overdose patient if a pattern of regular use has been established. A short-acting barbiturate may be given on a regular basis, after which the dosage is gradually reduced. Or alternatively, a long-acting barbiturate such as phenobarbital may be administered. The long-acting drug produces fewer behavioral problems and less chance of overdose. The signs of toxicity—such as slurred speech, rapid eye movements (known as nystagmus), and incoordination—are easy to observe, and the patient's dosage can be reduced accordingly.

After detoxification is accomplished psychiatric counseling is often necessary. Users of methaqualone and other sedatives may suffer an underlying depression, and it is during this period following detoxification when suicide attempts are most likely to occur. Antidepressant medication is sometimes necessary, and in many cases it is necessary to keep the extremely depressed patient in the hospital for two to three weeks while the medication begins to take effect. Finally, the detoxified patient should be educated about the fact that he or she has lost tolerance for the drug, and thus, if the previous dosage is again ingested it is likely that another overdose episode will result.

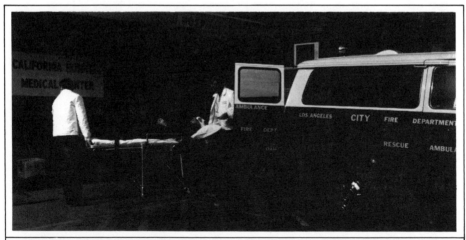

The U.S. Medical Examiner Reports stated that in 1981 there were 4,901 emergency-room mentions and 195 deaths related to methaqualone.

Jimi Hendrix, one of the most popular rock stars of the 1960s, died at the age of 28 when he choked on his own vomit after taking barbiturates, which slow the throat reflexes and depress respiration. Choking and vomiting, also characteristic of methaqualone, can make overdose treatment difficult.

CHAPTER 5

METHAQUALONE AND OTHER DRUGS

Methaqualone is structurally and functionally similar to the barbiturates and glutethimide, all of which are sedative/hypnotics. However, some of the barbiturates have additional uses, which include the treatment of convulsive disorders such as epilepsy. The barbiturates—amobarbital, tritabarbital, pentobarbital, phenobarbital, and secobarbital—are central nervous system depressants and have a history of being abused as "downers." They are capable of producing mild to moderate sedation, hypnosis, sleep, and deep coma.

The sedation produced by barbiturates varies with the dosage, the type of barbiturate, the route of administration, and the characteristics of the user. In addition, the barbiturates cause lethargy, fatigue, hangover, depression, and impaired judgment. Taken in combination with alcohol and other central nervous system depressants, these drugs can cause extreme intoxication or even death.

The barbiturates have been known to produce tolerance and dependence, which may be psychological and/or physical. Withdrawal can occur within 8 to 12 hours after the last drug. The symptoms include: weakness, anxiety, muscle twitching, insomnia, nausea, vomiting, fainting, weight loss, hallucinations, delirium, and seizures. More severe symptoms, such as grand mal seizures, may occur, and some patients withdrawing from barbiturates have died from cardiovascular collapse.

Glutethimide is also a central nervous system depressant related to the barbiturates and methaqualone. It produces sedation and sleep, and is primarily used to treat sleep difficulties. Glutethimide is only recommended for use for short periods of time—i.e., 3 to 7 days. It can cause drowsiness, sedation, incoordination, a feeling of inebriation, depression, and impaired judgment. There have been reports of tolerance, dependence, and residual sedation, or hangover. Withdrawal symptoms have been reported and include nausea, vomiting, nervousness, tremors, rapid heart rate, cramps, fever, and chills. Some individuals have experienced grand mal seizures.

Other drugs similar to methaqualone, barbiturates, and glutethimide include benzodiazepines (Valium, Dalmane, Librium, Restoril), chloral hydrate, hydroxyzine, meprobamate, and alcohol. These drugs vary in specific actions and therapeutic use, which may range from the treatment of anxiety and alcohol withdrawal to insomnia and symptomatic itching. However, they all have sedative/hypnotic actions and cause central nervous system depression, and thus have the potential for abuse.

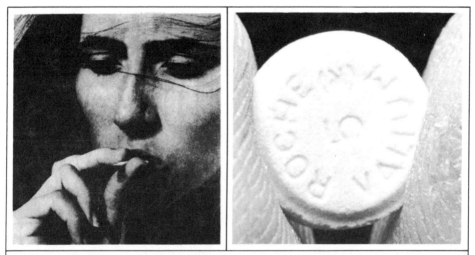

Alcohol and marijuana are often used in combination with methaqualone. The effects of these combinations are additive and can lead to delirium, coma, convulsions, pulmonary edema (excess fluid in the lungs), respiratory arrest, liver and kidney damage, and death. In fact, most methaqualone deaths are due to polydrug use.

Drugs Combined with Methaqualone

The only legally manufactured drug combination that included methaqualone was Mandrax. This drug, made in England, contained methaqualone and diphenhydramine, an antihistamine, and was used to treat insomnia. It has been found on the streets as an abused drug.

The most common drugs reported to be combined by street users of methaqualone are alcohol and/or marijuana. The effects of this combination are additive and can lead to increases in drowsiness, lack of coordination, and impaired judgment. The methaqualone/alcohol combination is most popular and is known as "luding out" (see Chapter 2). Since alcohol is also a central nervous system depressant, this combination is potentially very dangerous. It can depress respiratory function and more commonly causes severely impaired coordination and judgment, which can lead to serious accidents. This condition is especially dangerous to the individual taking the drug and to others with whom he or she comes into contact, because the individual using this combination of drugs may not be aware of how impaired his or her coordination and judgment are. Under these circumstances, therefore, death may be due to an accident in a motor vehicle or a drowning rather than to the direct action of the drugs on specific bodily functions.

Many fatal automobile accidents have been attributed to the effects of the alcohol/methaqualone combination.

Counterfeit methaqualone seized in Florida by the DEA. Much of the illegal methaqualone sold in the United States is flown aboard light aircraft into the southeastern states from Colombia.

CHAPTER 6

THE EXTENT OF
METHAQUALONE USE

Since 1975 the University of Michigan's Institute for Social Research has been collecting data to determine the extent of drug use among high school seniors in both public and private schools. Table 8 shows the percentage of those students who have used methaqualone.

When evaluating survey data one must keep in mind that often what is thought to be methaqualone is in fact not methaqualone at all. Analysis of street samples show that only 52% of the samples thought to be methaqualone actually contain the drug.

For methaqualone and for most drugs surveyed, the percent who ever used the drug is higher than the number who used it the previous year or month. This may be an indication that those students who began to use methaqualone in earlier grades have since discontinued use. The percent of those who used methaqualone in the previous year is a more accurate indicator of trends in current use. However, some of those who indicated methaqualone use in the previous year could also have used the drug earlier,

Table 8

Survey of High School Seniors Who Have Used Drugs of Abuse									
SURVEY GROUP	1975	1976	1977	1978	1979	1980	1981	1982	1983
Approximate number of students surveyed	9,400	15,400	17,100	17,800	15,500	15,900	17,500	17,700	16,300
Percent who ever used methaqualone	8.1	7.8	8.5	7.9	8.3	9.5	10.6	10.7	10.1
Percent who used methaqualone the previous year	5.1	4.7	5.2	4.9	5.9	7.2	7.6	6.8	5.4
Percent who used methaqualone the previous month	2.1	1.6	2.3	1.9	2.3	3.3	3.1	2.4	1.8
Percent daily users*	0	0	0	0	0	.1	.1	.1	0

*Daily is defined as drug use more than 20 times in the previous month.
SOURCE: University of Michigan's Institute for Social Research

therefore these figures do not reflect incidence of first use. If the question had been phrased "Did you take methaqualone for the first time within the last year?" the answer would reflect only new use.

A comparison of the percent of seniors who used methaqualone during the previous year with the percent who used it during the previous month reveals that most are using the drug either occasionally or on a one-time basis. The percent of seniors reporting monthly methaqualone use was less than half of those reporting use within the year, suggesting that most of the occasional users who reported use within a year did not develop a more regular pattern of use. Methaqualone use was still much lower than alcohol or marijuana use; of the 16,300 seniors in the 1983 survey, only 293 reported methaqualone use during the previous month, while 11,247 reported using alcohol and 4,401 reported using marijuana during the same time period. Almost none of the seniors questioned in 1983 used the drug daily, while about 897 used alcohol or marijuana daily. From Table 8 one can also conclude that methaqualone use, after a steady rise from 1978 to 1982, has been declining.

The use of methaqualone by seniors ranked 10th in 1983 after the use of alcohol, cigarettes, marijuana, stimulants, cocaine, sedatives, inhalants, tranquilizers, and hallu-

Table 9

Analysis of Methaqualone Use Reported by Emergency Rooms		
YEAR	1	2
1979	2,718	130,130
1980	4,700	131,115
1981	3,812	134,140
1982	3,018	136,392
1983	1,717	134,365

1 Based on emergency rooms reporting to DAWN at least 90% of the time

2 Based on all emergency rooms reporting to DAWN

SOURCE: National Institute on Drug Abuse

cinogens. Drugs used less frequently than methaqualone, ranked in order, were: barbiturates, opiates (other than heroin), LSD, PCP, and heroin.

Another source of information regarding the prevalence of methaqualone use is DAWN (the Drug Abuse Warning Network). DAWN conducted a five-year study which provided methaqualone trend data from 1979 to 1983. The

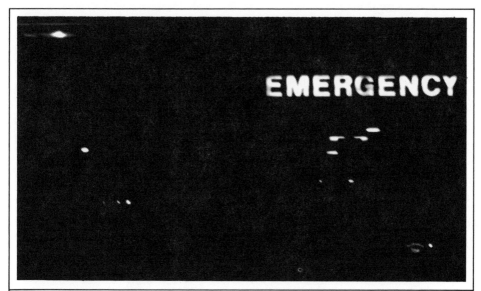

The Drug Abuse Warning Network reported that between 1982 and 1983 hospital emergency-room mentions of methaqualone declined slightly.

Table 10

Characteristics of Methaqualone Users	
SEX	
Male	56
Female	44
EDUCATION	
College-bound	38
Not college-bound	62
GEOGRAPHIC REGION	
Northeast	27
North central	25
South	28
West	20
POPULATION DENSITY	
High	31
Medium	36
Low	33
GRADE METHAQUALONE WAS	
FIRST USED	
6th	0
7th–8th	5
9th	18
10th	30
11th	30
12th	18
IN RESPONSE TO THE QUESTION:	
HOW MANY OF YOUR FRIENDS ARE	
TAKING QUAALUDES?	
None	64.5
Most or all	2.6

study is based upon reports from emergency rooms and coroners that over the five-year interval reported to DAWN at least 90% of the time (see Table 9). Because many hospitals drop in and out of the network, these figures are a low estimate of the total number of emergency room reports. Furthermore, these numbers do not reflect the widespread use of the drug since they do not include the great number of users who never enter the hospital. And finally, these individuals may have entered the emergency room for a nondrug-related problem, or for a problem resulting from poly-drug use.

Table 9 also shows the *total* number of emergency room mentions from 1979 to 1983. These data cannot be directly compared across years as different numbers of hospitals reported each year. Because of this variability in reporting, these figures are not predictive of trends, though they do emphasize the magnitude of medical problems related to methaqualone use.

Characteristics of Users

Of the 17,700 high school seniors reporting drug use in the study by the University of Michigan's Institute for Social Research, 1,894 (10.7%) had used methaqualone. Table 10 lists some characteristics of these users.

Between 1978 and 1980 sedative use rose among those not bound for college, barbiturate use dropped for both college-bound and noncollege-bound groups, and methaqualone use increased in both groups. As methaqualone use increased between 1978 and 1980 so did the proportion of seniors saying some of their friends used the drug. When the rate of methaqualone use declined after 1980, the trend in friends' use also declined.

In the 1960s and early 1970s college campuses gained an exaggerated reputation as places where drugs flowed freely.

After methaqualone became a Schedule I drug in 1984, any person caught with this drug could be fined and/or imprisoned for up to one year.

CHAPTER 7

THE LEGAL STATUS OF METHAQUALONE

When methaqualone was first introduced to the U.S. market in 1965 it was classified as a prescription drug, which meant that a physician had to write a prescription before an individual could obtain the drug. As long as the physician specified the quantity of tablets and the number of times the prescription could be refilled, there were no restrictions. At this time it was also possible to obtain the drug through a physician's verbal orders (i.e., over the telephone).

In 1973 methaqualone was reclassified as a Schedule II drug. Schedule II drugs include amphetamine and some narcotics. Restrictions placed on the manufacture and distribution of these drugs makes it much more difficult to obtain them than it is to obtain regular prescription drugs.

A Schedule II prescription (1) can only be ordered by a physician registered with the DEA; (2) must be in written form (verbal prescription orders are only allowed in emergencies and cannot provide more than a three-day supply); (3) is not refillable; and (4) can only provide for one month's supply. To be certified to prescribe these drugs the pharmacist must (1) work in a pharmacy registered with the DEA; (2) store Schedule II drugs in a locked cabinet; (3) use triplicate order forms to obtain the drug; (4) keep the prescription form in a separate file from other prescriptions; (5) maintain records of the exact amount received and dispensed; and (6) pass periodic audits by the DEA.

There are also rules and regulations placed on manufacturers of Schedule II drugs. Companies must keep exact records of the number of tablets made, distributed, returned, and lost during the manufacturing process. These records must be kept separate from all other company records. Also, each year the manufacturer and the U.S. attorney general's office agree on the specific quantity of tablets that can be produced. These are known as quotas and are based on the previous year's sales and disposal rate, and on the economy, the availability of raw materials, and national trends.

In 1982 Florida reclassified methaqualone as a Schedule I substance, and in 1984 the U.S. federal government took similar action. A Schedule I substance is considered to have a high potential for abuse and to have no accepted medical use. However, some Schedule I drugs may be used for research purposes by properly registered individuals. LSD, peyote, heroin, and marijuana are also Schedule I drugs. Placing methaqualone in Schedule I made it even less available than drugs in Schedule II.

A DEA chemist examines illegal methaqualone tablets to determine their source. Just as a bullet can be traced to the weapon from which it was fired, a tablet can be traced to the punch that manufactured it by a ballistics expert, who is able to interpret the microscopic marks made on the tablet by the particular punch used in the compression process.

Penalties for Trafficking and Use

Individuals who illicitly manufacture, distribute, or dispense a Schedule I or II substance in an unauthorized way are subject to severe penalties. First offenders may receive a prison term of not more than 5 years and/or a fine of not more than $25,000. Second offenders are subject to 10 years in prison and/or a $30,000 fine. These sentences refer to each count of criminal behavior. If a person is caught selling, manufacturing, or importing a drug, he or she may be convicted on several counts, and receive the appropriate penalties for each one.

Individuals who knowingly or intentionally possess a Schedule I or II substance without proof of a valid prescription are subject to not more than 1 year in prison and/or a fine of not more than $5,000. Persons violating this act for a second time are subject to not more than 2 years in prison and/or a $10,000 fine. There are additional and more severe penalties for persons who distribute these drugs to individuals under 21 years of age and for those who are involved in a continuing criminal enterprise. These penalties can double or triple the prison terms and fines for these individuals.

Police officers in Memphis, Tennessee, search the car of a suspected drug dealer (far left) whose merchandise included methaqualone.

Dr. George Gay directed the Haight-Ashbury Free Medical Clinic's Drug Detoxification, Rehabilitation, and Aftercare Project in the 1970s. Studies done at the clinic showed that methaqualone—which had been advertised as "harmless"—had addiction and overdose potential.

APPENDIX 1

CASE STUDIES OF METHAQUALONE USERS

Three case studies are presented to illustrate methaqualone dependence, withdrawal sickness, and overdose. They are abbreviated case histories taken from a survey of patients seen at the Drug Detoxification, Rehabilitation, and Aftercare Project of the Haight-Ashbury Free Medical Clinic in San Francisco. (A complete report was published in 1973 by Drs. Inaba, Gay, Newmeyer, and Whitehead in the *Journal of the American Medical Association,* Volume 224, pages 1505–1510.)

Methaqualone Dependence

A 20-year-old white male, with symptoms of persistent anxiety and insomnia, entered the clinic. He was a well-adjusted person who had completed high school and one year of college and who had satisfactory employment. He had a drug history of heavy cocaine and marijuana use during the previous two months and had tried a number of other drugs, but had not taken any repeatedly or often.

He was treated with diazepam (Valium) for anxiety and responded favorably to therapy. Subsequently, his counseling visits were reduced to once a month, and he reported only an occasional need for medication. However, two years later he reentered the clinic for daily therapy. He had begun taking methaqualone on social occasions. Although initially he was cautious and tried to restrict his use of the drug, over an 18-month period he had increased his dose to four or five 300-mg tablets a day, two or three times a week. Finally he began to use methaqualone daily and noticed that his tolerance had increased to the extent that five tablets plus alcohol still left him anxious.

The patient noted getting the shakes on one occasion and experiencing increased forgetfulness, anxiety, headache, and loss of appetite when he did not take methaqualone for a period of time. During the period of daily use he lost his job, his girlfriend, and his sexual abilities. He felt that he was no longer able to cope with his personal use of methaqualone. He was treated with diazepam, daily at first, and then the dose was gradually decreased until by the end of two weeks he was entirely off the medication. He remained drug free and in active counseling for at least the next six months.

Methaqualone Withdrawal Sickness

A 22-year-old white man was first seen at the clinic for a sodium pentobarbital (Nembutal) habit. He obtained a daily supply of "yellows" through legal prescriptions from a physician. He appeared at the clinic because of his concern about the difficulty and dangers involved with "kicking barbs." His drug history during the previous two months consisted of infrequent use of heroin, frequent use of cocaine, alcohol, and methaqualone, and heavy daily use of pentobarbital and marijuana.

He was treated in an outpatient detoxification program with phenobarbital, a long-acting barbiturate. Following his initial treatment he reappeared at the clinic with barbiturate withdrawal symptoms—high blood pressure, high temperature, slightly higher heart rate, sweating, and extreme anxiety and hyperactivity. He also complained of a restless night's sleep and nausea. The dose of phenobarbital was increased and then gradually tapered off over the next two weeks. He continued to receive active psychosocial counseling at the clinic.

After about six months the patient requested daily counseling. He had been unable to quench his desire for the depressant euphoria he obtained from the barbiturates, and his friends had recommended Quaaludes. He had thus begun taking methaqualone—300 mg five to eight times a day for the previous two months. He bought the tablets from a friend who had a legal prescription.

Apparently convinced by reports of the "nonaddicting" nature of the drug, he attempted to stop taking methaqualone. He experienced the same symptoms as he had with barbiturate withdrawal—nervousness, tremors, and insomnia. He then elected to decrease his methaqualone intake under supervision and counseling, and within two weeks he

had succeeded. However, he continued to use methaqualone recreationally, and remained concerned about his persistent need to abuse sedative/hypnotic drugs.

Methaqualone Overdose

A 21-year-old white woman entered the clinic after a three-
year period of heroin addiction. She had overdosed five
times in the last three years. The patient was counseled and
treated daily for opiate withdrawal symptoms, and after she
stopped using heroin she obtained a job and returned to the
clinic for periodic aftercare counseling.

About six months later she was brought into the clinic
in a stuporous state. She did not respond well to painful
stimuli, her breathing was slow, irregular, and shallow, and
her heart rate was high. She was given a drug to increase her
respiratory rate and depth, and she regained a near normal
level of responsiveness during the next two to three hours,
during which time she was under close observation and
supportive care.

During recovery the patient recalled the events leading
to her overdose. She reported that she was despondent and
depressed over the loss of her job, and she took between
four and ten 300-mg tablets of methaqualone. She then
walked to a local bar and had a few drinks. She could not
remember anything until she found herself at the clinic.
After the methaqualone/alcohol overdose, she did not respond well to counseling and returned to her heroin habit.

Drug abusers are often
willing to try just about any
drug that might provide a
momentary high. When
inhaled, amyl nitrate, a
liquid added to diesel fuel to
raise the octane number,
produces a brief but intense
"rush."

APPENDIX 2

STATE AGENCIES FOR THE PREVENTION AND TREATMENT OF DRUG ABUSE

ALABAMA
Department of Mental Health
Division of Mental Illness and
  Substance Abuse Community
  Programs
200 Interstate Park Drive
P.O. Box 3710
Montgomery, AL 36193
(205) 271-9253

ALASKA
Department of Health and Social
  Services
Office of Alcoholism and Drug
  Abuse
Pouch H-05-F
Juneau, AK 99811
(907) 586-6201

ARIZONA
Department of Health Services
Division of Behavioral Health
  Services
Bureau of Community Services
Alcohol Abuse and Alcoholism
  Section
2500 East Van Buren
Phoenix, AZ 85008
(602) 255-1238

Department of Health Services
Division of Behavioral Health
  Services
Bureau of Community Services
Drug Abuse Section
2500 East Van Buren
Phoenix, AZ 85008
(602) 255-1240

ARKANSAS
Department of Human Services
Office on Alcohol and Drug Abuse
  Prevention
1515 West 7th Avenue
Suite 310
Little Rock, AR 72202
(501) 371-2603

CALIFORNIA
Department of Alcohol and Drug
  Abuse
111 Capitol Mall
Sacramento, CA 95814
(916) 445-1940

COLORADO
Department of Health
Alcohol and Drug Abuse Division
4210 East 11th Avenue
Denver, CO 80220
(303) 320-6137

CONNECTICUT
Alcohol and Drug Abuse
  Commission
999 Asylum Avenue
3rd Floor
Hartford, CT 06105
(203) 566-4145

DELAWARE
Division of Mental Health
Bureau of Alcoholism and Drug
  Abuse
1901 North Dupont Highway
Newcastle, DE 19720
(302) 421-6101

DISTRICT OF COLUMBIA
Department of Human Services
Office of Health Planning and
  Development
601 Indiana Avenue, NW
Suite 500
Washington, D.C. 20004
(202) 724-5641

FLORIDA
Department of Health and
  Rehabilitative Services
Alcoholic Rehabilitation Program
1317 Winewood Boulevard
Room 187A
Tallahassee, FL 32301
(904) 488-0396

Department of Health and
  Rehabilitative Services
Drug Abuse Program
1317 Winewood Boulevard
Building 6, Room 155
Tallahassee, FL 32301
(904) 488-0900

GEORGIA
Department of Human Resources
Division of Mental Health and
  Mental Retardation
Alcohol and Drug Section
618 Ponce De Leon Avenue, NE
Atlanta, GA 30365-2101
(404) 894-4785

HAWAII
Department of Health
Mental Health Division
Alcohol and Drug Abuse Branch
1250 Punch Bowl Street
P.O. Box 3378
Honolulu, HI 96801
(808) 548-4280

IDAHO
Department of Health and Welfare
Bureau of Preventive Medicine
Substance Abuse Section
450 West State
Boise, ID 83720
(208) 334-4368

ILLINOIS
Department of Mental Health and
  Developmental Disabilities
Division of Alcoholism
160 North La Salle Street
Room 1500
Chicago, IL 60601
(312) 793-2907

Illinois Dangerous Drugs
  Commission
300 North State Street
Suite 1500
Chicago, IL 60610
(312) 822-9860

INDIANA
Department of Mental Health
Division of Addiction Services
429 North Pennsylvania Street
Indianapolis, IN 46204
(317) 232-7816

IOWA
Department of Substance Abuse
505 5th Avenue
Insurance Exchange Building
Suite 202
Des Moines, IA 50319
(515) 281-3641

KANSAS
Department of Social Rehabilitation
Alcohol and Drug Abuse Services
2700 West 6th Street
Biddle Building
Topeka, KS 66606
(913) 296-3925

KENTUCKY
Cabinet for Human Resources
Department of Health Services
Substance Abuse Branch
275 East Main Street
Frankfort, KY 40601
(502) 564-2880

LOUISIANA
Department of Health and Human
  Resources
Office of Mental Health and
  Substance Abuse
655 North 5th Street
P.O. Box 4049
Baton Rouge, LA 70821
(504) 342-2565

MAINE
Department of Human Services
Office of Alcoholism and Drug
  Abuse Prevention
Bureau of Rehabilitation
32 Winthrop Street
Augusta, ME 04330
(207) 289-2781

MARYLAND
Alcoholism Control Administration
201 West Preston Street
Fourth Floor
Baltimore, MD 21201
(301) 383-2977

State Health Department
Drug Abuse Administration
201 West Preston Street
Baltimore, MD 21201
(301) 383-3312

MASSACHUSETTS
Department of Public Health
Division of Alcoholism
755 Boylston Street
Sixth Floor
Boston, MA 02116
(617) 727-1960

Department of Public Health
Division of Drug Rehabilitation
600 Washington Street
Boston, MA 02114
(617) 727-8617

MICHIGAN
Department of Public Health
Office of Substance Abuse Services
3500 North Logan Street
P.O. Box 30035
Lansing, MI 48909
(517) 373-8603

MINNESOTA
Department of Public Welfare
Chemical Dependency Program
  Division
Centennial Building
658 Cedar Street
4th Floor
Saint Paul, MN 55155
(612) 296-4614

MISSISSIPPI
Department of Mental Health
Division of Alcohol and Drug Abuse
1102 Robert E. Lee Building
Jackson, MS 39201
(601) 359-1297

MISSOURI
Department of Mental Health
Division of Alcoholism and Drug
  Abuse
2002 Missouri Boulevard
P.O. Box 687
Jefferson City, MO 65102
(314) 751-4942

MONTANA
Department of Institutions
Alcohol and Drug Abuse Division
1539 11th Avenue
Helena, MT 59620
(406) 449-2827

NEBRASKA

Department of Public Institutions
Division of Alcoholism and Drug Abuse
801 West Van Dorn Street
P.O. Box 94728
Lincoln, NB 68509
(402) 471-2851, Ext. 415

NEVADA

Department of Human Resources
Bureau of Alcohol and Drug Abuse
505 East King Street
Carson City, NV 89710
(702) 885-4790

NEW HAMPSHIRE

Department of Health and Welfare
Office of Alcohol and Drug Abuse
 Prevention
Hazen Drive
Health and Welfare Building
Concord, NH 03301
(603) 271-4627

NEW JERSEY

Department of Health
Division of Alcoholism
129 East Hanover Street CN 362
Trenton, NJ 08625
(609) 292-8949

Department of Health
Division of Narcotic and Drug Abuse
 Control
129 East Hanover Street CN 362
Trenton, NJ 08625
(609) 292-8949

NEW MEXICO

Health and Environment Department
Behavioral Services Division
Substance Abuse Bureau
725 Saint Michaels Drive
P.O. Box 968
Santa Fe, NM 87503
(505) 984-0020, Ext. 304

NEW YORK

Division of Alcoholism and Alcohol
 Abuse
194 Washington Avenue
Albany, NY 12210
(518) 474-5417

Division of Substance Abuse
 Services
Executive Park South
Box 8200
Albany, NY 12203
(518) 457-7629

NORTH CAROLINA

Department of Human Resources
Division of Mental Health, Mental
 Retardation and Substance Abuse
 Services
Alcohol and Drug Abuse Services
325 North Salisbury Street
Albemarle Building
Raleigh, NC 27611
(919) 733-4670

NORTH DAKOTA

Department of Human Services
Division of Alcoholism and Drug
 Abuse
State Capitol Building
Bismarck, ND 58505
(701) 224-2767

OHIO

Department of Health
Division of Alcoholism
246 North High Street
P.O. Box 118
Columbus, OH 43216
(614) 466-3543

Department of Mental Health
Bureau of Drug Abuse
65 South Front Street
Columbus, OH 43215
(614) 466-9023

OKLAHOMA
Department of Mental Health
Alcohol and Drug Programs
4545 North Lincoln Boulevard
Suite 100 East Terrace
P.O. Box 53277
Oklahoma City, OK 73152
(405) 521-0044

OREGON
Department of Human Resources
Mental Health Division
Office of Programs for Alcohol and
  Drug Problems
2575 Bittern Street, NE
Salem, OR 97310
(503) 378-2163

PENNSYLVANIA
Department of Health
Office of Drug and Alcohol
  Programs
Commonwealth and Forster Avenues
Health and Welfare Building
P.O. Box 90
Harrisburg, PA 17108
(717) 787-9857

RHODE ISLAND
Department of Mental Health,
  Mental Retardation and Hospitals
Division of Substance Abuse
Substance Abuse Administration
  Building
Cranston, RI 02920
(401) 464-2091

SOUTH CAROLINA
Commission on Alcohol and Drug
  Abuse
3700 Forest Drive
Columbia, SC 29204
(803) 758-2521

SOUTH DAKOTA
Department of Health
Division of Alcohol and Drug Abuse
523 East Capitol, Joe Foss Building
Pierre, SD 57501
(605) 773-4806

TENNESSEE
Department of Mental Health and
  Mental Retardation
Alcohol and Drug Abuse Services
505 Deaderick Street
James K. Polk Building, Fourth Floor
Nashville, TN 37219
(615) 741-1921

TEXAS
Commission on Alcoholism
809 Sam Houston State Office Building
Austin, TX 78701
(512) 475-2577

Department of Community Affairs
Drug Abuse Prevention Division
2015 South Interstate Highway 35
P.O. Box 13166
Austin, TX 78711
(512) 443-4100

UTAH
Department of Social Services
Division of Alcoholism and Drugs
150 West North Temple
Suite 350
P.O. Box 2500
Salt Lake City, UT 84110
(801) 533-6532

VERMONT
Agency of Human Services
Department of Social and
  Rehabilitation Services
Alcohol and Drug Abuse Division
103 South Main Street
Waterbury, VT 05676
(802) 241-2170

VIRGINIA
Department of Mental Health and
  Mental Retardation
Division of Substance Abuse
109 Governor Street
P.O. Box 1797
Richmond, VA 23214
(804) 786-5313

WASHINGTON
Department of Social and Health
  Service
Bureau of Alcohol and Substance
  Abuse
Office Building—44 W
Olympia, WA 98504
(206) 753-5866

WEST VIRGINIA
Department of Health
Office of Behavioral Health Services
Division on Alcoholism and Drug
  Abuse
1800 Washington Street East
Building 3 Room 451
Charleston, WV 25305
(304) 348-2276

WISCONSIN
Department of Health and Social
  Services
Division of Community Services
Bureau of Community Programs
Alcohol and Other Drug Abuse
  Program Office
1 West Wilson Street
P.O. Box 7851
Madison, WI 53707
(608) 266-2717

WYOMING
Alcohol and Drug Abuse Programs
Hathaway Building
Cheyenne, WY 82002
(307) 777-7115, Ext. 7118

GUAM
Mental Health & Substance Abuse
  Agency
P.O. Box 20999
Guam 96921

PUERTO RICO
Department of Addiction Control
  Services
Alcohol Abuse Programs
P.O. Box B-Y Rio Piedras Station
Rio Piedras, PR 00928
(809) 763-5014

Department of Addiction Control
  Services
Drug Abuse Programs
P.O. Box B-Y Rio Piedras Station
Rio Piedras, PR 00928
(809) 764-8140

VIRGIN ISLANDS
Division of Mental Health,
  Alcoholism & Drug Dependency
  Services
P.O. Box 7329
Saint Thomas, Virgin Islands 00801
(809) 774-7265

AMERICAN SAMOA
LBJ Tropical Medical Center
Department of Mental Health Clinic
Pago Pago, American Samoa 96799

TRUST TERRITORIES
Director of Health Services
Office of the High Commissioner
Saipan, Trust Territories 96950

Further Reading

Hartmann, Ernest. *The Sleeping Pill.* New Haven: Yale University Press, 1978.

Hollister, Leo E. *Clinical Pharmacology of Psychotherapeutic Drugs.* New York: Churchill Livingstone, Inc., 1983.

Hughs, Richard and Brewin, Bob. *Tranquilizing of America: Pill-Popping & the American Way of Life.* New York: Harcourt Brace Jovanovich, Inc., 1979.

Mendelson, Wallace B. *The Use & Misuse of Sleeping Pills: A Clinical Guide.* New York: Plenum Publishing Company, 1980.

Young, Lawrence A., et al. *Recreational Drugs.* New York: Berkley Publishing Corp., 1982.

Glossary

addiction   a condition caused by repeated drug use, including a compulsive urge to continue using the drug, a tendency to increase the dosage, and physiological and/or psychological dependence

adulterate   to dilute a drug either with an inert material to add bulk or another drug to alter the effects of the original drug

amphetamines   drugs that stimulate the nervous system, generally used as mood elevators, energizers, antidepressants, and appetite depressants

anesthetic   a drug that produces loss of sensation and/or loss of consciousness

antihistamine   a drug that inhibits the action of histamine and thus reduces the allergic response

antipsychotic drug   a drug that calms a patient who is in a psychotic state

ataxia   incoordination

barbiturates   drugs that cause depression of the central nervous system, generally used to reduce anxiety or to induce euphoria

depersonalization   a feeling of being outside oneself and observing one's behavior, rather than actually experiencing it

dose   amount of drug taken, usually measured in quantity of drug per body weight, or mg/kg

drug   any substance—plant, powder, solid, fluid, or gas—that when ingested, injected, sniffed, inhaled, or absorbed from the skin affects bodily functions

drug dependence   a state in which drug taking serves as a reward for the behavior which precedes it; or a condition defined by a strong need to repeatedly experience the drug effect even in the absence of physical dependence

drug interaction   a change in the action of one drug due to earlier or simultaneous administration of another drug

euphoria   a mental high characterized by a sense of well-being

hallucination   a sensory impression that has no basis in external stimulation

heroin   a semisynthetic opiate produced by changing the chemical structure of morphine

ketamine   a surgical anesthetic similar to, but much less potent than, PCP

marijuana   a mixture of the leaves, flowers, buds, and branches of the plant *Cannabis sativa,* which, when ingested, produces psychoactive effects

methylenedianaline   a substance, often found as a contaminant in methaqualone, that causes liver damage

morphine   the principal psychoactive ingredient of opium, producing sleep or a state of stupor, and used as the standard against which all morphine-like drugs are compared

necrotizing cystitis   a serious condition that affects the bladder and is characterized by nausea, vomiting, and frequent, painful, and bloody urination

opiate   a compound from the milky juice of the poppy plant, *Papaver somniferum,* including opium, morphine, codeine, and their derivatives, such as heroin

overdose   when more of a drug is taken than the amount necessary to obtain a desired effect, usually resulting in adverse effects or even death

paresthesia   tingling of a part of the body, such as the fingers, lips, or tongue

PCP   the psychoactive drug phencyclidine, or angel dust

pharmacology   the study of drugs and their effects on living organisms

physical dependence   an adaption of the body to the presence of a drug, such that its absence produces withdrawal symptoms

placebo   a pill, tablet, or liquid that has no pharmacologically active ingredients but may be made to look like a drug and is used in experiments or to satisfy a patient's medication-taking desire

potency   a measure of a drug's activity in terms of how much of the drug is needed to produce a given effect; the lower the amount required to produce the effect, the more potent the drug

psychedelic drug   a drug that produces hallucinations or has mind-altering or mind-expanding properties (e.g., LSD, mescaline, and peyote)

psychoactive drug   a drug that alters mood, behavior, or

thought processes

psychological dependence a condition in which the drug user craves a drug to maintain a sense of well-being and feels discomfort when deprived of it

sedative-hypnotic drug a drug that produces a general depressant effect on the nervous system, such as relaxation, relief from anxiety, and sleep

side effect a drug effect that is secondary to the major, desired effect of the drug

tolerance a physical and/or behavioral adaptation to the drug such that larger amounts are required to produce the original effects, or such that a fixed amount produces decreasing effects over time

toxic effect a drug-induced effect that temporarily or permanently damages the cells or organ systems

tranquilizer a drug that has calming, relaxing effects

withdrawal the physiological and psychological effects of discontinued usage of a drug

Index

Marilyn Carroll, Ph.D., is an experimental psychologist who specializes in psychopharmacology. For the last six years she has conducted research on oral drug dependence for the National Institute on Drug Abuse. Widely published in many leading journals, Dr. Carroll received her Ph.D. in psychology from Florida State University and is currently an assistant professor in the department of psychiatry at the University of Minnesota.

Gary R. Gallo, M.S., is the director of the University of Minnesota Drug Information Service in Minneapolis, Minnesota. The Service is affiliated with the Department of Pharmacy at the University of Minnesota Hospitals and the College of Pharmacy where Mr. Gallo is also an assistant professor. Mr. Gallo received a B.S. in biology from the University of Wisconsin-Madison, a B.S. in pharmacy from the Massachusetts College of Pharmacy-Boston, and an M.S. in hospital pharmacy from the University of North Carolina-Chapel Hill.

Solomon H. Snyder, M.D., is Distinguished Service Professor of Neuroscience, Pharmacology and Psychiatry at The Johns Hopkins University School of Medicine. He has served as president of the Society for Neuroscience and in 1978 received the Albert Lasker Award in Medical Research. He has authored *Uses of Marijuana, Madness and the Brain, The Troubled Mind, Biological Aspects of Mental Disorder,* and edited *Perspective in Neuropharmacology: A Tribute to Julius Axelrod.* Professor Snyder was a research associate with Dr. Axelrod at the National Institutes of Health.

Barry L. Jacobs, Ph.D., is currently a professor in the program of neuroscience at Princeton University. Professor Jacobs is author of *Serotonin Neurotransmission and Behavior* and *Hallucinogens:Neurochemical, Behavioral and Clinical Perspectives.* He has written many journal articles in the field of neuroscience and contributed numerous chapters to books on behavior and brain science. He has been a member of several panels of the National Institute of Mental Health.

Jerome H. Jaffe, M.D., formerly professor of psychiatry at the College of Physicians and Surgeons, Columbia University, has been named recently Director of the Addiction Research Center of the National Institute on Drug Abuse. Dr. Jaffe is also a psychopharmacologist and has conducted research on a wide range of addictive drugs and developed treatment programs for addicts. He has acted as Special Consultant to the President on Narcotics and Dangerous Drugs and was the first director of the White House Special Action Office for Drug Abuse Prevention.